Economic Policy
in Eastern Europe

Economic Policy in Eastern Europe

Were Currency Boards a Solution?

Edited by
ILIANA ZLOCH-CHRISTY

PRAEGER

Westport, Connecticut
London

Library of Congress Cataloging-in-Publication Data

Economic policy in Eastern Europe : were currency boards a solution? / edited by Iliana Zloch-Christy.
p. cm.
Includes bibliographical references and index.
ISBN 0–275–96858–8 (alk. paper)
1. Europe, Eastern—Economic policy—1989– 2. Currency boards—Europe, Eastern. I. Zloch-Christy, Iliana, 1953–
HC244.E24336 2000
332.4'947—dc21 99–088507

British Library Cataloguing in Publication Data is available.

Library of Congress Catalog Card Number: 99–088507
ISBN: 0–275–96858–8

First published in 2000

Praeger Publishers, 88 Post Road West, Westport, CT 06881
An imprint of Greenwood Publishing Group, Inc.
www.praeger.com

Printed in the United States of America

The paper used in this book complies with the Permanent Paper Standard issued by the National Information Standards Organization (Z39.48–1984).

10 9 8 7 6 5 4 3 2 1

To I.K.H.

Contents

Figures and Tables

FIGURES

TABLES

Preface

Iliana Zloch-Christy

This book is based on contributions by Eastern European and Western scholars to one of the most interesting issues of current economic policy in the transition countries and former centrally planned economies in Eastern Europe—the financial arrangement of currency boards. I have been fascinated by the challenges to economic policy in postcommunist Eastern Europe and Russia, since these countries are undertaking the greatest reconstruction job in history. In this regard the question whether economic policy has a desired effect on the economic development of a country and in our study whether currency boards have such an effect is a challenging issue to be analyzed. Some of the chapters in the book were presented at the International Studies Association annual meetings in Washington, D.C., February 16–20, 1999. However, my goal as editor has been to produce an integrated and coherent book, and I do hope that readers will react positively to this attempt in their judgment of how far I have succeeded.

As in my previous books I tried to invite as many female colleagues as possible to participate, and I (again) failed to realize that because the women in our profession have been and remain a considerable minority—this applies for Eastern European and Western countries, and particularly for the small Central European country, Austria, where I happened to live. I completed the book during my scholarship at Harvard University, where I benefited from the fascinating atmosphere of knowledge and reason. I would like to acknowledge the stimulating discussions with Richard N. Cooper. Steve Rosefielde read carefully the first version of the manuscript and as always in the last 15 years gave me his stimulating remarks. I know that Steve appreciates my devotion and love on the work on a new manuscript. I hope this will continue and the present book will not be my last one. Finally a word of thanks to my daughter Daniela Christy, who was also a source of inspiration to begin and to complete this study.

Introduction

Iliana Zloch-Christy

One of the most fascinating issues of contemporary world economic development is the transition process in the former Soviet Union and Eastern Europe.[1] The challenges to the economic policy in this region are of particular interest to economists, political scientists, and social scientists. Strategies of economic policy and institution building in post-communist Eastern Europe with a focus on currency board arrangements are the subject of this book. It will focus on the question of whether the currency board is a solution to the economic problems of the countries that have adopted it and to the challenges of economic transformation. The analysis is in historical and comparative perspectives with such regimes in a few Asian and Latin American countries. Every attempt is made to keep our approach to the discussion positive.

The main questions addressed are:

1. What are the main problems and challenges of economic transition in postcommunist Eastern Europe?
2. What are the main economic policy strategies in Eastern Europe and Russia?
3. What are the main challenges to the economies that adopted currency boards?
4. Were currency boards a solution?

In preparing the study I have invited the participation of colleagues who hold a wide range of views and belong to different nationalities: Bulgaria, Estonia, Poland, Finland, and the United States.

The book is organized into two parts. The first part addresses the challenges to economic policy in Eastern Europe. It includes contributions from the Polish scholar Grzegorz W. Kolodko, former first deputy prime minister and minister of finance of Poland (1994–97), on economic policy and the importance of institution building; and from the American scholar and Harvard economist Richard N. Cooper on the issue of currency convertibility in the transforming economies in comparative perspective with the experience of Western European countries after World War II. Part II turns specifically to a discussion of currency board arrangements and includes the following contributions: the Finnish economists Iikka Korhonen, Niina Pautola, and Pekka Sutela, and I address the question, Why currency boards?; Niina Pautola discusses currency boards in international perspective; Iikka Korhonen and Pekka Sutela attempt to analyze the macroeconomic impact of the currency boards in the two Baltic states—Estonia and Lithuania; the Estonian economists Mart Sörg and Vello Vensel focus specifically on Estonia's experience after introducing the currency board in 1992; a chapter based on my work on the currency board in Bulgaria takes a critical perspective on the economic consequences of failed reforms in this small southeastern European country. The conclusion summarizes the main findings of the study and analyzes what we have learned.

NOTE

1. The terms *Eastern Europe, postcommunist (socialist) Europe, transition economies, transforming economies,* and *former centrally planned economies* are used as synonyms. Eastern Europe is defined in political rather than geographical terms, namely, the former Soviet Union and the European countries that were under Soviet domination after 1945. The term *Baltic countries* includes the three former Soviet republics, Estonia, Lithuania, and Latvia. The terms *West, Western countries,* and *developed economies* are used to designate the economies that comprise the membership of the OECD. Please refer also to the individual authors' descriptions of the countries involved in their analyses.

Abbreviations

BIS	Bank for International Settlements
BOE	Bank of Estonia
CB	currency board
CE	Central Europe
CEEC	Central and East European countries
CEFTA	Central European Free Trade Agreement
CIS	Commonwealth of Independent States
CMEA	Council for Mutual Economic Assistance
CPE	centrally planned economy
EBRD	European Bank for Reconstruction and Development
EFTA	European Free Trade Association
EIB	European Investment Bank
EU	European Union
EPU	European Payments Union
FDI	foreign direct investment
GDP	gross domestic product
GNP	gross national product

IBRD	International Bank for Reconstruction and Development (The World Bank)
ILO	International Labor Organization
IMF	International Monetary Fund
NGOs	Nongovernmental organizations
OECD	Organization for Economic Cooperation and Development
UN	United Nations
WTO	World Trade Organization

PART I

ECONOMIC POLICY IN POSTCOMMUNIST EASTERN EUROPE

1

Challenges of Economic Policy in Postcommunist Transition

Grzegorz W. Kolodko

This chapter attempts to analyze the challenges to economic policy in Eastern Europe. The main problems and challenges of transition can be summarized as follows. The acute (short- and long-term) *problems* are evidenced most clearly by the deep recession (sharp declines in investments and savings), high unemployment, financial crisis (huge budget deficits, no clear fiscal strategy, and external debt), low productivity, breakdown of trade with the former trading partners, and last but not least nationality conflicts. Actually it should be stressed here that the great slump in Eastern Europe (with a partial exception of Poland, Hungary, and the Czech Republic) suggests that instead of using the term *deep recession*, one should use *true depression.*

The problems of transition indicate three main *challenges* for the postcommunist economies and societies:

1. stabilizing the economy (without being obsessed with *targeting monetary aggregates*), coming out of the deep depression, and, urgently, avoiding long-term unemployment;
2. achieving a more efficient use of resources;
3. improving the prospects for better long-term economic growth performance with special attention being paid to institution building.

All of this suggests that the Eastern European countries should clearly define their strategies of how to deal with the above-mentioned problems and challenges and to create the necessary macroeconomic environment for changes in investment, savings, labor, and management. The challenges to economic policy makers in the Eastern countries with their inexperienced economic and political elites (which in many cases have been acting with arrogant incompetence) and to the Western advisers and financiers have been enormous.

Let's turn to our detailed discussion of the problems and challenges of transition. The centrally planned economy has ceased to exist. Even in countries still considered socialist (communist), such as China and Vietnam, the mechanism of economic coordination has shifted to a great extent from state intervention to market allocation. Thus, during the 1990s the process of postsocialist transformation advanced significantly. About thirty countries in Eastern Europe, the former Soviet Union, and Asia are undergoing vast systemic changes. Undoubtedly, these changes are leading to full-fledged market economies, although the precise outcome of transformation is not going to be the same for all countries involved. Whereas some, leaders in transition and well-placed geopolitically, are bound to join the EU in the foreseeable future, others, lagging behind in systemic changes, will remain hybrid systems with the remnants of central planning alongside elements of market regulation and a growing private sector. Whereas some countries will expand quickly and catch up with their developed neighbors within a generation, others will experience sluggish economic growth and a relatively low standard of living.

Transition to a market economy is a lengthy process comprised of various spheres of economic activities. New institutional arrangements are of key importance for successful transformation. A market economy requires not only liberal regulation and private ownership, but also adequate institutions. For this reason transition can be executed only in a gradual manner, since institution building is a gradual process based upon new organizations, new laws, and the changing behavior of various economic entities. The belief that a market economy can be introduced by "shock therapy" has been wrong, and in several cases, when attempted, has caused more problems than it has solved. Only liberalization and stabilization measures can be introduced in a radical manner, and even this is not a necessity. The need for such methods depends on the scope of financial destabilization and is only possible under certain political conditions.

The main argument in favor of transition was a desire to put the countries in question on the path of sustainable growth. It was assumed that the shift of property rights from state to private hands and the shift of allocation mechanisms from state to free market would soon enhance saving rates and capital formation, as well as allocative efficiency, and also contribute to high-quality growth. Unfortunately, for a number of reasons this has not occurred. In all transition economies, before any growth has occurred (and in some countries there is no growth yet) there has been severe contraction, ranging from 20 percent over three years in Poland to over 60 percent in nine years in Ukraine (Table 1.1). These unfavorable results are the consequence of both the legacy of the previous system and the policies exercised during transition, although it is obvious that the latter are of major importance.

These policies were based to a large extent on the so-called Washington consensus. The set of policies designed along this line has been stressing the importance of liberalization, privatization, and the opening of postsocialist economies as well as the necessity of sustaining financial discipline. However, having been developed for another set of conditions, initially this approach was missing crucial elements necessary for systemic overhaul, stabilization, and growth. These elements included institution building, improvement of corporate governance of the state sector prior to privatization, and the redesign of the role of the state, instead of its urgent withdrawal from economic activities. The incorrect assumption that emerging market forces can quickly substitute for the government in its role in new institutional setup, investment in human capital, and development of infrastructure, has caused severe contraction and growing social stress.

The need to manage the institutional aspects of transition has been recognized and addressed only in later stages. The technical assistance of the IMF and the World Bank in dealing with these issues may have an even more important positive influence on the course of transition and growth than their financial involvement. Lending by these organizations is often called "assistance," despite the fact that these are just commercial credits with tough accompanying terms. They are having the consequence of enforcing far-reaching structural reforms and pushing toward policies that are supposed to bring durable growth.

Hence, there is a need to search for a new consensus about policy reforms necessary for sustained growth. The East Asian contagion, East European transition, and Brazilian crisis suggest that for recovery and durable growth healthy financial fundamentals and liberal, transparent

Table 1.1
Recession and Growth in the Transition Economies, 1990–97

Countries	Years of GDP Decline	Did GDP Fall after Some Growth?	Average Annual Rate of GDP Growth			1997 GDP Index (1989 = 100)	Rank
			1990–93	*1994–97*	*1990–97*		
Poland	2	no	−3.1	6.3	1.6	111.8	1
Slovenia	3	no	−3.9	4.0	0.0	99.3	2
Czech Republic	3	yes*	−4.3	3.6	−0.4	95.8	3
Slovakia	4	no	−6.8	6.3	−0.3	95.6	4
Hungary	4	no	−4.8	2.5	−1.1	90.4	5
Uzbekistan	5	no	−3.1	−0.3	−1.7	86.7	6
Romania	4	yes	−6.4	2.1	−2.2	82.4	7
Albania	4	yes	−8.8	4.9	−2.0	79.1	8
Estonia	5	no	−9.7	4.1	−2.8	77.9	9
Croatia	4	no	−9.9	3.0	−3.4	73.3	10
Belarus	6	no	−5.4	−2.6	−4.0	70.8	11
Bulgaria	6	yes	−7.4	−3.6	−5.5	62.8	12
Kyrgyzstan	5	no	−9.3	−2.4	−5.8	58.7	13
Kazakhstan	6	no	−6.7	−6.0	−6.3	58.1	14
Latvia	4	yes	−13.8	2.2	−5.8	56.8	15
Macedonia	6	no	−12.9	−0.8	−6.9	55.3	16
Russia	7	yes*	−10.1	−5.3	−7.7	52.2	17
Turkmenistan	7	no	−4.5	−12.5	−8.5	48.3	18
Lithuania	5	no	−18.3	0.5	−8.9	42.8	19
Armenia	4	no	−21.4	5.4	−8.0	41.1	20
Azerbaijan	6	no	−14.5	−5.7	−10.1	40.5	21
Tajikistan	7	no	−12.2	−8.4	−10.3	40.0	22
Ukraine	8	no recovery	−10.1	−12.1	−11.1	38.3	23
Moldova	7	yes*	−12.6	−10.2	−11.4	35.1	24
Georgia	5	no	−24.1	2.9	−10.6	34.3	25

*GDP contracted again in 1998.

Source: National statistics, international organizations, and the author's own calculations.

deregulation are not the only decisive factors. Sound institutional arrangements, reregulation of financial markets, and wise government policy are also essential. Over the recent experience with the crises of several emerging markets (including the ones in transition countries), the outline of a new consensus—a post-Washington consensus—can be drawn. It points not only to the need for liberal markets and open economies, but stresses the new role of the state, the fundamental meaning of market organizations and the institutional links between them, and the need for more equitable growth.

After losing over a quarter of GDP between 1990 and 1998, the majority of the postsocialist transition economies are gaining momentum. If this is not yet true in the two most sizable (Russia and Ukraine), they too have the chance to become growing economies (Kolodko 1998). In the coming years, the postsocialist emerging markets will become not only rapidly growing economies, but—owing to the East Asian turmoil—the fastest growing region in the world. Yet how fast this growth is going to be depends on policy reforms implemented in particular countries. The direction of these reforms will also depend on cooperation with international organizations and their technical advice and financial support, which are conditionally linked to execution of market-friendly policies and implementation of sound structural reforms. Thus these organizations' influence upon the course of reforms and chosen policies is much stronger than their actual financial engagement and undertaken risk.

POLICY WITHOUT GROWTH: MISSING ELEMENTS

From the mid-1980s to the beginning of the 1990s the Washington consensus was accepted as common wisdom on policies for movement from stabilization to growth. It was assumed that tough financial policy accompanied by deregulation and trade liberalization would be sufficient to conquer stagnation and launch economic growth, especially in the less developed countries toward which the Washington consensus was addressed. Despite the fact that the policy reforms advised by this line of thought were at the time mostly relevant to the Latin American experience, they were applied to structural crisis issues in other regions, including transition economies. Later, there was an interaction between theories and practice, a process of learning by doing. On the one hand, the orientation of these policy reforms has had an important influence on the course of postsocialist transition. On the other hand, the transition process has had an impact on policy as well.

A summary of the 1989 Washington consensus was given by John Williamson (1990), who named the proposed set of policies, stressing the importance of the organizations involved. He enumerated ten points which at the time seemed to be agreed on by influential financial organizations, political bodies, and professional economists:

- Fiscal Discipline. Budget deficit . . . should be small enough to be financed without recourse to the inflation tax. . . .
- Public Expenditure Priorities. Expenditure should be redirected from politically sensitive areas . . . toward neglected fields with high economic returns and the potential to improve income distribution. . . .
- Tax Reform. Tax reform involves broadening the tax base and cutting marginal tax rates. The aim is to sharpen incentives and improve horizontal equity without lowering realized progressivity. . . .
- Financial Liberalization. The ultimate objective of financial liberalization is market-determined interest rates, but experience has shown that, under conditions of a chronic lack of confidence, market-determined rates can be so high as to threaten the financial solvency of productive enterprise and government. . . .
- Exchange Rates. Countries need a unified (at least for trade transactions) exchange rate set at a level sufficiently competitive to induce a rapid growth in nontraditional exports and managed so as to ensure exporters that this competitiveness will be maintained in the future.
- Trade Liberalization. Quantitative trade restrictions should be rapidly replaced by tariffs, and these should be progressively reduced until a uniform low tariff in the range of 10 percent (or at most around 20 percent) is achieved. . . .
- Foreign Direct Investment. Barriers impeding the entry of foreign firms should be abolished; foreign and domestic firms should be allowed to compete on equal terms.
- Privatization. State enterprises should be privatized.
- Deregulation. Governments should abolish regulations that impede the entry of new firms or that restrict competition, and then

should ensure that all regulations are justified by such criteria as safety, environmental protection, or prudential supervision of financial institutions.

- Property Rights. The legal system should provide secure property rights without excessive costs and should make such rights available to the informal sector. (Williamson 1997, pp. 60–61)

Later, mainly under the influence of the experience of overhauling the Latin American economies over the first half of the 1990s and taking into consideration the lessons learned from Eastern Europe and the former Soviet Union, the new agenda was presented. Whereas it includes obvious points from earlier thoughts, there are new concerns and accents. Again, ten points were raised:

- Increase saving by (inter alia) maintaining fiscal discipline
- Reorient public expenditure toward (inter alia) well-directed social expenditure
- Reform the tax system by (inter alia) introducing an eco-sensitive land tax
- Strengthen banking supervision
- Maintain a competitive market exchange rate
- Pursue intra-regional trade liberalization
- Build a competitive market economy by (inter alia) privatizing and deregulating (including the labor market)
- Make well-defined property rights available to all
- Build key institutions such as independent central banks, strong budget offices, independent and incorruptible judiciaries, and agencies to sponsor productivity missions
- Increase educational spending and redirect it toward primary and secondary schools. (Williamson 1997, p. 58)

The new items on this agenda correctly address the issues of institution building, environmental protection, and investment in education, yet they are still missing some important points that are especially pertinent to transition economies. First of all, dealing with corporate governance reform in the state sector before privatization is not mentioned, nor is the behavioral aspect of institution building. Also the necessity of equitable growth is still overlooked. The shortest point on the agenda of the early Washington consensus, that is, "Privatization. State enterprises should be privatized," is in reality a long-term policy challenge. Even if there is a sound commitment to privatize quickly and extensively—which is not always the case—it is not feasible, for both technical and political reasons. There are also the issues of sequencing, pace, distribution of costs and benefits, and the efficient exercise of corporate governance.

As for the institutional aspect of reform, in postcommunist transition economies, unlike in distorted developing market economies, it is not enough merely to establish organizations, such as an independent central bank or comprehensive tax administration. Cultural changes are also necessary to facilitate efficiency and growth—changes in behavior within organizations and changes in the interactions between them.

The early Washington consensus was actually aiming at countries that already had market economies, and were not just in transition to such a system. Joseph Stiglitz (1998a), while stressing the importance of governments as a complement to markets, points out that the consensus achieved in the late 1980s and early 1990s among the United States Treasury, the IMF, and the World Bank, as well as some influential think tanks, was catalyzed by the experience of Latin America in the 1980s. He claims that for this reason countries facing different challenges have never found satisfactory answers to their most pressing questions in the Washington consensus. Its simplified interpretation vis-à-vis the postcommunist economies implied that it would be sufficient to fix the appropriate financial fundamentals and privatize the bulk of state assets. Subsequently, growth should begin and continue for the long term. Because this has not happened as presumed, the Washington consensus should be reconsidered.

There has always been a question as to the actual existence of a Washington consensus. Was a consensus achieved, or was the effort just an intention and well-motivated attempt? In fact, the latter is the case. "There is no standard terminology for these sets of doctrines, and various practitioners advocated these doctrines with varying degrees of subtlety and emphasis. The set of views is often summarized as the 'Washington consensus,' although to be sure, there never was a consensus even in Washington (let alone outside Washington) on the appropriateness of these policies" (Stiglitz 1998b, p. 58).

The partial failure of the Washington consensus with regard to transition economies must be linked with the neglect of the significance of *institution building* for the beginning of growth, even if economic fundamentals are by and large in order. Such oversight explains why so many Western scholars initially did not properly understand the real problem. Institutions change slowly, but they have a strong influence on economic performance. As D. North, the 1993 Nobel Laureate in Economics, states, since

> Western neo-classical economic theory is devoid of institutions, it is of little help in analyzing the underlying sources of economic performance. It would be little exaggeration to say that, while neo-classical theory is focused on the operation of efficient factor and product markets, few Western economists understand the institutional requirements essential to the creation of such markets since they simply take them for granted. A set of political and economic institutions that provides low-cost transacting and credible commitment makes possible the efficient factor and product markets underlying economic growth. (North 1997, p. 2)

Expectations of growth were based on the assumption that market institutions, if they had not yet appeared automatically, would somehow rise up soon after liberalization and stabilization measures were executed. It was believed that if policies were put in place to secure the progress of stabilization and enhance sound fundamentals, the economy should regain momentum and start to develop quickly. However, what actually happened was much more depressing. Because of a vacuum with neither plan nor market system, productive capacity was utilized even less than previously, savings and investments began to decline, and instead of fast growth there was deep recession. A lack of institutional development turned out to be the missing element in transition policies based on the Washington consensus. Instead of sustained growth, liberalization and privatization without a well-organized market structure led to extended contraction and slump. This was not only the legacy of a socialist past, but also the result of current policies.

Under some circumstances, although not in every case, the manner of reasoning characteristic of the Washington consensus may be relevant to the challenges faced by distorted, less developed market economies. Contrary to the experience of postsocialist economies, in these cases certain market organizations have always been in place. In postsocialist countries, however, organizations essential to a market economy were either distorted or did *not* exist, so the economy could not expand. Some institutions had to be developed from scratch, since they did not exist under the centrally planned regime. As a result, even with progress in liberalization and radical privatization, there was still no positive supply response. Misallocation of resources and investments continued, although this time for different reasons.

At the outset of transition the only relatively developed part of a market infrastructure was a commodities trading network, but even this was operating under chronic shortages. A capital market structure was nonexistent. The lack of financial intermediaries discouraged accumulation and worsened allocation of savings. Thus, immediately after the collapse of communism, the lack of proper regulation of the emerging capital market and the dearth of such key organizations as investment banks, mutual funds, a stock exchange, a security control commission, and so on, caused distortions that could not be offset by liberalization and privatization.

All these organizations and institutional links must be developed gradually. Considering the point of departure, this also calls for a process of retraining many professionals to enable them to work in the market environment. This takes years, and thus it would be much wiser to manage the processes of liberalization and privatization at a pace compatible with the speed of human capital development. Otherwise, loosed market forces will not be able to shape economic structures and processes and raise competitiveness and ability for growth. A dissonance between liberalization measures and institution building has actually occurred in a number of countries that took a more radical approach to transition. In these cases "creative destruction," popular in Poland at the beginning of the 1990s, failed to deliver, because there was too much destruction and not enough creation.

The Eastern European countries were full- or overfull-employment economies, that is, economies with labor shortages. Thus a social security system protecting against unemployment did not exist, because it was not needed. All countries in this region have had to develop such a safety net from scratch.[1] In the meantime, before such systems could be implemented, in addition to the misallocation of capital, there has been the misallocation of labor.

Since the mid-1990s, the Bretton Woods organizations (the World Bank and the IMF) have started to pay more attention to the way market structures are organized as well as to the behavioral aspects of market performance. A number of less developed and transition economies learned quickly that there is no sustained growth without sound fundamentals. Later, it was learned and accentuated, that the market and growth need both *liberalization* and *organization*. Now, due to the experience of transitional contraction and because of conclusions drawn from the East Asian crisis, we learn that even with sound fundamentals—a balanced budget and current account, low inflation, a stable currency, liberalized trade, and a vast private sector—there will not be sustained growth if these favorable features are not supported by an appropriate *institutional setup*. Actually, without such a setup, the fundamentals themselves will become unsound and unsustainable, what time has proved by the actual developments, for instance, in the Czech Republic or more recently in Brazil.

There seems to be a growing agreement that the early Washington consensus must be revised and adjusted to actual challenges and new circumstances. If it is going to work, elements missing thus far must be included. These elements are linked with institutional arrangements, although they are not universal. Some elements were missing regarding the overhaul of the Latin American debt crisis, others in the case of counteracting Eastern Asia's contagion, and still others in fighting the Eastern European transitional depression. In the latter, eight elements are of key importance:

- The lack of organizational infrastructure for a liberal market economy.
- Weak financial intermediaries unable to allocate efficiently privatized assets.
- A lack of commercialization of state enterprises prior to privatization.
- Unqualified management unable to execute sound corporate governance under the conditions of a deregulated economy.
- A lack of institutional infrastructure for competition policy.
- A weak legal framework and judiciary system, and a consequent inability to enforce tax codes and business contracts.
- Poor local government unprepared to tackle the issues of regional development.
- A lack of NGOs supporting the functioning of the emerging market economy and civil society.

All this indicates that policies that under other conditions may have worked were not effective in overcoming the crisis in the postsocialist economies. Even if the targets and instruments as such were well defined, they could not be reached and used as envisaged, since they were put into use within a *systemic vacuum*.

TOWARD A NEW CONSENSUS

Rather than a permanent agreement between principal partners, the process of developing a new consensus should involve a constant search for such agreement as well as a quest for new partners. These features are indispensable for ultimate success. From time to time, when the situation changes and our knowledge about it evolves, new documents and programs, accentuating additional points of concern and examining old points in a different light, come to the fore. A good example of such progress is the World Bank's 1996 Annual Development Report, devoted entirely to the transition from plan to market (World Bank 1996), and the September 1996 IMF Interim Committee Declaration on a *Partnership for Sustainable Global Growth* (IMF 1996).

The latter may be seen as a modified version of the early Washington consensus. Among eleven points, six are of special relevance to the situation of transition economies. Point 1 stresses that monetary, fiscal, and structural policies are complementary and reinforce each other. Point 3 claims that there is a need to create a favorable environment for private savings. Point 7 accentuates that budgetary policies have to aim at medium-term balance and a reduction in public debt, while point 9 says that structural reforms must be supplemented with special attention paid to the labor markets. Point 10 stresses the importance of good corporate governance, and point 11 cautions against corruption in the public sector and money laundering in the banks, warning that their monitoring and supervision must be strengthened. Other points, also important for sustainable development, address the issues of exchange rate stability, disinflation, resisting protectionist pressure, progress toward increased freedom of capital movement, and fiscal adjustment by reducing unproductive spending while ensuring adequate investment in infrastructure.

However, the Washington consensus is not an official position taken by any particular organization or institution. It is rather a gathering of policy options being agreed on by important partners to such an extent that the agreement may be considered a consensus. Yet there is still a search for agreement between the organizations as well as among the policy makers, policy-oriented researchers, and advisers. The author was personally involved in all three—research, advice giving, and policy making—and it was quite interesting for me to receive a response to the outcome of my involvement from John Williamson,[2] who has stressed that

> I was particularly pleased that you have tried to define an alternative to big bangery in terms of a more careful design of individual policy components rather than generalized go slow ("gradualism").[3] On just about all the individual items you identify, certainly including protection and privatization, I agree with you in retrospect, and indeed I would have agreed with you at the time. . . . But in all honesty I have to confess that I still worry that had I been in the place of Balcerowicz (who was the minister of finance in Poland in 1989–91) I might not have put together the decisive package that I think in retrospect Poland needed at the time, and that laid the foundation for your successful period in office. Perhaps one needed a little bit of overkill to make it emotionally possible for your allies to accept that the world had changed, and even to give you the opportunity of correcting their excesses and in the process winning their acceptance of the new model? It reminds me of the situation in my home country: I am much more comfortable with Tony Blair than with Mrs. Thatcher, but I am not sure that we could have had him without her.

This time, psychological and political rather than economic and financial arguments are given as decisive factors favoring the radical set of policies undertaken at the beginning of the 1990s. Nonetheless, it seems that we still differ as far as the evaluation of the scope and costs of that overkill. Was it only "a little bit" of otherwise necessary measures, as one may still believe, or was it a serious excess of unnecessary radicalism, as it seems to be proved elsewhere (Kolodko 1991; Nuti 1992; Rosati 1994; Poznanski 1996; Hausner 1997)?

When ideas and strategies involving more gradual change and the active involvement of the state in institutional redesign in postsocialist transition economies were expounded for the first time (Kolodko 1989, 1992; Nuti 1990; Poznanski 1993), and when they were later implemented in Poland (Kolodko 1993, 1996, 1999), they were unorthodox and controversial with respect to the Washington consensus. In fact, these new ideas did not so much endorse more gradual change, but recognized that the necessary changes would be time-consuming by their very nature. In 1997 and 1998, however, even in official international circles, there were widespread signs that a new consensus was emerging, and that it was, to a certain extent, based on the ideas implemented in Poland in 1994–97 (Kolodko and Nuti 1997). Thanks to its multitrack approach, Poland is now recognized to have avoided the adverse experience of other transition economies. The new ideas and policies, developed under the "Strategy for Poland," were to some extent elaborated against the mainstream of the early Washington consensus and have now contributed importantly to its revision.

In the aftermath of the Southeast Asian crisis, as it has spread beyond anybody's expectation, the train of thought has also begun to change track among the most influential opinion leaders in the international financial community. This has been accompanied by a much belated beginning of doubt raised regarding the accuracy of the recipe proposed for postcommunist emerging markets, especially for the most important, Russia. A consensus has not yet been agreed on, but lessons are gradually being learned. It is now admitted that

> the benefits brought by short-term international lenders are questionable: they do not provide new technology; they do not improve the management of domestic institutions; and they do not offer reliable finance of current account deficit. In countries with high savings rates, they also increase already excessive investment rates. To manage the inflows, borrowers may have to accumulate huge reserves. . . . The Asian saga proves, once again, that liberalization of inadequately regulated and capitalized financial system is a recipe for disaster. (Wolf 1998, p. 23)

All the while, the Bretton Woods organizations were insisting upon and determining their financial involvement based on tough fiscal and monetary policy. If it was a period of 10 percent GDP decline, or a period of 10 percent expansion, there was always pressure to bring the fiscal gap down and keep the real interest rate up. Even when the budget deficit was smaller than that of industrial countries and the real interest rate was so high that it was not possible to contain the deficit further due to soaring costs of servicing the public debt, there was a permanent requirement on continuing fiscal and monetary tightness. High real interest rate facilitates portfolio investors (through the interest rate differentials), but at a cost to both taxpayers and the business sector owing to a crowding-out effect.

The importance of a change in corporate governance—as opposed to a sheer transfer of property titles—is now being recognized even by early keen supporters of rapid, mass privatization. There is no clear evidence that the privatized enterprises perform better than state enterprises in the aftermath of privatization. Nicholas Stern (1996, p. 8), who has been top manager at an international institution, points to the process of restructuring, which "itself will be a major and fundamental task involving investment, hard decisions and dislocation. It will be much less painful if economic growth, effective corporate governance and well-functioning safety nets are established." Thus good corporate governance of public enterprises and sound competition policy are at least as essential for recovery as privatization and liberalization.

After the laissez-faire of the early transition, values of cooperation and solidarity are being rediscovered. Even billionaire financier George Soros has not hesitated to admit that "Although I have made a fortune in the financial markets,[4] I now fear that the untrammeled intensification of laissez-faire capitalism and the spread of market values into all areas of life is endangering our open and democratic society. . . . Too much competition and too little cooperation can cause intolerable inequities and instability" (Soros 1997, p. 72). It should be obvious from the outset that transition based on a sort of laissez-faire must bring "intolerable inequities and instability"; yet it is still not acknowledged widely enough and such an obvious conclusion is still challenged.

The 1996 *World Development Report* emphasizes strongly the need for social consensus, although it will be difficult to reach, considering falling output and growing inequality in transition economies. "Establishing a social consensus will be crucial for the long-term success of transition—cross-country analyses suggest that societies that are very unequal in terms of income, or assets tend to be politically and socially less stable and to have lower rates of investment and growth" (World Bank 1996, p. 42).

It is now generally accepted that in economies still affected by structural rigidities, such as formal and informal indexation and sluggish supply response, once inflation has fallen well below a threshold of about 20 percent, attempts at speeding up disinflation could have significant, perhaps intolerable costs—as for instance in Romania in 1998–99. What counts is that inflation should continue to fall steadily and noticeably, without ever accelerating again. Such a process of disinflation contributes not only to growing credibility of the government and monetary authorities, but secures the predictability of economic developments and creates a better business environment and confidence on the international scene.

The prerequisite for an enhanced savings ratio (i.e., faster than income increase) is a growth of real income, stabilization, and optimistic expectations. Only against such a background can the propensity to save steadily increase. The 1996 EBRD *Transition Report*, which is devoted to infrastructure and savings, stresses the equal role of increasing government savings—especially through the overhaul of social security and pension systems, and more broadly based taxation at lower rates—and the development of contractual savings and life insurance. From this perspective, the pressure for high and positive real interest rates has been grossly misplaced. The fiscal and quasi-fiscal activities of central banks, notably in the emerging economies and especially in postsocialist countries, have attracted considerable attention (Fry 1993). In particular, the costs of sterilization policies, which are the result of excessive interest rate differentials or of undervalued currencies, have come to the fore (e.g., the OECD country study of the Czech Republic—1996). It turns out that for a considerable time, the central banks of both the Czech Republic and Poland have wasted about one percent of GDP in their sterilization policies (Nuti 1996, p. 3).

There is yet one more key feature of the emerging consensus. This time, along with the continuous leading role of the IMF and the World Bank, it must encompass more partners. Other international organizations, like the UN, OECD, WTO, ILO, and EBRD, should play a bigger role than they have thus far. Also, regional organizations in Asia, CEFTA in Central Europe, or the CIS in the former Soviet Union, should be better prepared to present their purpose in the global forum and try to influence the process of changing the international financial and economic order. Some international NGOs ought to be more influential too.

Thus the search for the new consensus must rely not only on the quest for new policies agreed on in Washington, but also on the policies Washington and other important places in different parts of the global economy share. There are many hints that such a process is on the way, but there is much more yet to be accomplished.

THE MEANS AND ENDS OF ECONOMIC POLICY

The lack of success of policies based on the early Washington consensus is also due to the confusion of the means of the policies with their ends. A sound fiscal stance, low inflation, a stable exchange rate, and overall financial stabilization are only the means of economic policy, while sustained growth and a healthier standard of living are its ends.

Yet after several years of exercising these policies, neither growth nor a higher standard of living has been achieved in transition countries. Important changes like privatization and liberalization are merely instruments, not targets. So it is strange that so often these instrumental processes are presented as a core of economic policy, if not its ultimate end. Too much attention is focused on the means that hypothetically should lead to improvement of efficiency and competitiveness, instead of concentration on the outcome of these exercises. Such bias leads to policy distortion and the tools become the goals themselves, without sufficient concern about their impact on the real economy.

In economic policy sometimes it happens that intellectual oversimplification assumes that, from a certain point and under certain circumstances, things should run themselves, so there is no need to think about how to manage them. An extreme example of such thought is the supposition that "the best policy is no policy."[5] But, considering the distinction between ends and means, it should be obvious to all those involved in economic research, advice, and policy, that such confusion cannot be explained merely by the naiveté and laziness of economists and politicians. Actually, they do work hard. The intellectual misunderstandings result from political antagonism, and the difference is more about conflicts of interests than about alternative theoretical concepts and scientific explanations.

Of course, it does happen that policy mistakes occur due to a lack of experience and proper knowledge, but more often this confusion stems from adherence to a particular group of interests, or to "theoretical schools," that happen to be ideological and political lobbies too. This is why there are no leftist or rightist doctors or engineers, but there are leftist and rightist economists and policy makers. John Williamson (1990) points to a "political" Washington and a "technocratic" Washington, stressing their different priorities and policy options. However, there are important divisions not only *between* the political and technocratic parts of Washington, but also *within* them.

What makes the picture still more complex is the fact that some of the actors on the so-called technocratic side of the scene do play, even if unintentionally, political roles as well. This is also true with regard to the Bretton Wood organizations, especially the IMF. Their influence and the consequences of their policies simply have such serious implications for particular countries and regions, if not the entire global economy, that sometimes they have much more to say—and decide—than what may be seen as purely technocratic concerns. The position of the IMF toward big transition countries like Russia and Ukraine are the best cases in point here.

But the issue is even more complex, because—aside from intellectual controversies and different normative values—there are also different political, economic, and financial interests involved. Otherwise it would be impossible to interpret why erroneous policies had continued, in many cases, even after it was obvious that they were wrong. These were the cases, for instance, with early liberalization and stabilization policy in Poland in 1989–92, the neglect of corporate governance in the Czech Republic in 1993–96, the Russian privatization of 1994–98, executed with the active involvement of politically connected informal institutions, and with fraudulent Albanian financial intermediaries in 1995–97, which were tolerated until the whole economy eventually collapsed.

Such events serve only as examples of the confusion of economic policy's targets with its instruments. Economic policy is not to be judged by the pace of privatization, but by its efficiency, measured first by the increase of competitiveness and budgetary proceeds, and then by the increase in contribution to national income. The strong insistence on privatization's acceleration coming from some lobbies and their political allies is merely a means of selling the assets cheaper. Thus there are entities that are able to buy these assets not faster, as is publicly suggested through political connections and dependent news media, but to acquire them cheaper than under a more reasonably paced procedure. The ones that sell fast, sell cheap too. And the ones who buy fast, buy cheap as well.

There have been warnings, criticisms, and intellectual and political opposition against all these unwise policies, but still they have gotten through. Why? It has occurred not due to a lack of good economic ideas or a deficit of sound policy programs, but because of pressure from strong lobbies and interest groups. Therefore, in designing good policy, it is important not only to be right but also to be able to enforce the preferred policies. Often it happens that the strongest lobby is not where there is truth and logic, but where there is power and money.

Therefore, true reforms, those that facilitate the public interests of many as opposed to the particular interests of a few, must always be thought of as a means to long-term targets, that is, sustained growth. Otherwise, there will be fictitious "progress" reflected in an artificial improvement of a given situation. If the share of the private sector, the scope of trade liberalization, or the deregulation of capital transfers is bigger than it would be without these policies, but at the same time economic contraction is deeper or growth more sluggish and the standard of living is deteriorating, then the overall situation is worse, not better. Yet, often, economic status is judged from the perspective of a particular interest group, which is presented as a picture of the general economic situation.

So, while evaluating the actual standing of an economy and policy, one must consider not only what is examined, and by what means it is scrutinized, but also who is carrying out such an evaluation. With this in mind, it is obvious that, for instance, the evaluations of Moody's rating agency and Russian trade unions must be as different as the interests of the Morgan Stanley investment bank and Siberian miners.

Hence, the aims of development policy are more comprehensive and their interpretation is changing as well among those who subscribed to the Washington consensus, primarily the World Bank. Not only should a balanced economy and sustained growth be of serious policy concern, but also standard of living improvement, distribution of income, the environment, and, last but not least, democracy itself. "Our understanding of the instruments to promote well-functioning markets has also improved, and we have broadened the objectives of development to include other goals, such as sustainable development, egalitarian development, and democratic development" (Stiglitz 1998a, p. 1). True, the World Bank has always been inclined toward social issues and development of human capital, unlike other international financial institutions, particularly other banks. Usually banks look to profits, not to the human development index, as an indicator of their success. It must be acknowledged that the World Bank has become involved in a number of projects that serve to increase standards of living and decrease poverty, and not only in transition economies.

Yet now even the IMF is trying to join the club and claim that it too would like to aim at a more fair distribution of the fruits of growth, if only the advised policies would deliver some. Stanley Fischer, the IMF first deputy managing director, concerned about equitable growth for a long time, has raised the question, Why do equity considerations matter for the Fund? And then he has answered that

> first, as a matter of social justice, all members of society should share in the benefits of economic growth. And although there are many important arguments about precisely what constitutes a fair distribution of income, we accept the view that poverty in the midst of plenty is not socially acceptable. But, second, there is also an

> instrumental argument for equity: adjustment programs that are equitable and growth that is equitable are more likely to be sustainable. These are good enough reasons for the IMF to be concerned about equity considerations—whether it be poverty reduction or concerns about income distribution in the programs the IMF support. (Fischer 1998, p. 1)

Undoubtedly, the experience of transformation has contributed significantly to these changes. We still have to deal with the difficult road from contraction to growth in postsocialist economies, but we have also experienced fast growth in Asian reformed socialist economies, which—unlike the Eastern European and the former Soviet Union transition economies—did not follow many early Washington consensus suggestions. Now these experiences, together with the aftermath of the Southeast Asian crisis and its contagion, are working as a catalyst for the emergence of "the post-Washington consensus" the same way that the Latin American debt crisis of the 1980s ignited the formation of its predecessor. However, there is still a long distance to travel from the emerging intellectual consensus to a real political agreement about appropriate policy reforms and actions. And, of course, even if intellectual consensus is closer than before, controversies regarding different normative values and contradictory interests remain.

TRANSITION AS A PROCESS OF SYSTEMIC REDESIGN

The only chance for the ultimate success of transformation is to design suitable institutions, which often must be developed from the very beginning. This design is more difficult in post-Soviet republics than in Eastern Europe, because in the former there was a lack of even such basic institutions as a sovereign central bank or national currency, and private property as the means of production was virtually nonexistent. Particularly in the former Soviet Asian economies the process is going at a much slower pace and yet it also is directed at further liberalization and opening up.

As for Eastern Europe, some countries have taken a course of gradual, perhaps even too slow liberalization and privatization. Although that was followed by relatively milder GDP contraction, it caused a delay of crucial structural reforms as well. Nevertheless, if the necessary time is devoted to appropriate institution building, it can pay off later. If, however, the time of gradual liberalization is wasted from the perspective of institutional reforms, then the chance for a long-term expansion is indeed weak.

Although under these circumstances contraction was more severe in early stages, later, institution building is often more advanced. In the long run, after learning the bitter lesson that market economies do not expand without a wise, government-led development policy and well-designed institutions, both types of economies, European and former Soviet economies in transition as well as the reformed economies of China and Vietnam, have a chance to succeed in their market endeavors.

Government involvement in the process of comprehensive institution building is of vital importance. Truly, this, as much as liberalization, is the essence of transition. In other words, without taking adequate care of institutional arrangements, liberalization and privatization is unable to deliver what the nations expect from their economies. Thus, if the state fails to design a proper institutional setup, then market failures prevail and informal institutionalization takes over. Instead of a sound market, in the words of the chief economists of the World Bank and the European Bank of Reconstruction and Development, a "bandit capitalism" emerges.

> It is easy to identify institutional arrangements that work well: each partner does what it is supposed to do, there is good coordination, little conflict and the economy grows smoothly and rapidly. We can also recognise ill-functioning institutional arrangements: change is inhibited by bureaucratic requirements or there is "bandit capitalism" with pervasive corruption and deceit. (Stern and Stiglitz 1997, p. 20)

Such institutional pathologies could arise as a result of *transition-by-chance*, as opposed to *transition-by-design.* In several cases inaccurate transition policy has led to such adversity. A system where "only the stupid pay taxes," contracts are not executed as agreed, or payments are not made on time, is hardly a market economy. It is rather chaos stemming from institutional disintegration.

Without the knowledge of how a new system works, and without a vision of how to get to that system, there is no way to accomplish the target on time and in good shape. Transition becomes protracted: costs are higher than necessary, while results are not as good as they could be under an alternative scenario, and the whole process lasts longer than would otherwise be necessary. And, as was stressed by the advocates of transition-by-design contrary to the supporters of transition-by-chance, the recession lasts longer, recovery comes later, and output expands more slowly (Poznanski 1996). Thus the proper institutional design is a paramount task during the time of transition. At the same time, its accomplishment is more difficult than elsewhere, because of institutional discontinuity. The old setup (for instance, central price regulation, or the investment's allocation by Gosplan [the Soviet central planning authority] and branch ministries) does not work anymore, and the new one (for instance, investment banking, or stock exchange) is not yet in place. Thus systemic vacuum prevails.

A foundation for market capitalism requires the dominance of private property, but also a competitive enterprise sector, functioning markets, and respect for the rules of market allocation. Well-performing financial intermediaries are necessary to facilitate trade transactions and investment deals, as well as to promote savings. But the market, its introduction notwithstanding, also needs a proper legal environment, one that is able to support execution of market rules, enforcement of contracts, and the correct behavior of economic agents (firms, households, organizations, and the government). For these reasons transition calls not for a dismissal of government, but for its streamlining and adjustment to the new circumstances. The World Bank, unlike the advocates of market fundamentalism, admits that

> the state makes a vital contribution to economic development when its role matches its institutional capability. But capability is not destiny. It can and must be improved if governments are to promote further improvements in economic and social welfare. . . . Three interrelated sets of institutional mechanisms can help create incentives that will strengthen the state's capability. These mechanisms aim to:
>
> - Enforce rules and restraints in society as well as within the state,
> - Promote competitive pressures from outside and from within the state, and
> - Facilitate voice and partnership both outside and within the state. (World Bank 1997, p. 38)

This is true for all economic systems, countries with differing scopes of economic activity, various GDP levels, and odd institutional advancement, so it is even truer for transition economies. In countries where the rules were previously fundamentally different from current postsocialist regulations, the introduction of new behaviors and the enforcement of new regulations for economic entities call for even harder and more determined state effort than elsewhere.

Unfortunately, the state's ability to attack the issue of law enforcement is much weaker during transition than it was under state socialism. It is also weaker than under the governments of traditional market economies, with mature civil societies and well-working institutions. Postsocialist states have been deliberately weakened by neo-liberal policies, often led with the official support of the governments of leading industrial countries and international organizations.

For example, in the author's judgment the Russian government is weak and unable to collect taxes not because of the legacy from the communist period, but owing to an ill-advised liberal approach and wrong deregulation and privatization. Now it is difficult to bring things under the sovereignty of the new state, because they have been allowed to get out of control of the old state, mainly because of mismanaged liberalization and the manner in which institutional redesign occurred.

As for new partnerships between market players, that is precisely what gradual institution building is about. In the long term, such partnerships enhance the environment for growth, but in the initial stages ongoing changes can destabilize existing links between partners involved in economic activities. The old relationships cease to exist, while the new ones are weak. Thus active state participation is needed, since market relations are often associated with inappropriate events owing to activities of various lobbies and informal organizations, including organized crime.

TRANSITION AS AN INSTRUMENT OF DEVELOPMENT STRATEGY

The new institutional setup must be founded on the basis of new organizations that did not exist (since they were not needed) under the centrally planned state economy. Transition calls not only for a new legal system, but also for learning a new type of behavior. Enterprises, banks, the civil service and state bureaucracy, even households—all of them must quickly learn how to perform under the circumstances of the new reality of the emerging market system. Political leaders in postsocialist countries do not have, as in ancient time Moses did, forty years to turn their people around. To accelerate this process and cut the costs of institutional and cultural adjustment require special training and education efforts by political and intellectual elites and NGOs. The Bretton Woods institutions are contributing to this acceleration. After seeing that providing new skills and knowledge is sometimes more important than just lending money, they have started to pay much more attention to technical assistance and professional training.

In countries that enjoyed a relatively liberal system under socialism (for example, Poland and Hungary), the process of learning goes much faster. If there was already a private sector and decentralized management of state companies, learning new methods of corporate governance is smoother. If there was already a two-tier banking system, learning sound commercial banking is easier. If there was already an anti-trust body, this previously relatively useless organization (because of the shortages) now must regulate well-supplied markets to make them truly competitive.

In countries that had traditional centrally planned regimes until the late 1980s, learning is slower. This factor explains the differences in the economic performance of such neighbors as Hungary and Romania. The faster the process of institution building proceeds, the better the environment for business activity and hence for growth becomes. Government guidance and intervention can hasten the whole process, as in Poland in the 1990s, but if mismanaged, as it was over the same period of time in Russia, can spoil it too. Nonetheless, such a risk cannot be an excuse for state withdrawal from these activities. The risk calls for wise guidance and rational intervention.

In the very long term, the transition should be seen as a major instrument of development policy. Systemic changes that do not lead to durable growth and sustainable development do not make sense. However, there are ideologically motivated efforts at change, which are made without deep concern about their pragmatic implications for society. Such motivation must not be neglected since it can be strong, especially during a period of revolutionary change. And the postcommunist transformations are of such a nature, regardless of their pace.

Yet the situation is more complex, because behind political motivations there are always interest groups. To counterbalance these interests with lobbies oriented toward long-range progress and development is not easy, since such a group would need to resist strong pressures coming from interest groups. In other words, if there are lobbies fighting with such determination and force in favor of their own present interests, there are no lobbies fighting with such determination in favor of long-term development and remote policy targets. Actually, the only visible and somewhat effective lobby of the latter type is the environmental lobby.

However apparent it is that systemic transition is not the target but merely the path to a more important goal, there is still some confusion on this point. This confusion is first about the interdependence of institutional changes and real economy expansion. Can the system be perfect while growth is not satisfactory, or can it be praised at a time when ability to expand is weak? Of course it should not, yet peculiarly, it often is. It is apparent in professional discourse that reforms are appreciated for their own sake, without paying enough attention to their real outcome.

Thus the enormous contraction in Eastern Europe and the former Soviet Union has been a result of, on the one hand, deficiencies of development policy and exaggeration of the significance of transition as such and, on the other, a confusion of transition with liberalization and privatization. Policies have focused mainly on stabilization measures, trade liberalization, and privatization, without paying enough attention to events in the real economy, such as output, consumption, investment, unemployment, and the like. This approach changed the initial conditions (although not always for the better) and caused contraction instead of growth.

From a very long-term development viewpoint, the system's design plays an instrumental role in expansion and development. As one generation passes away, the next takes its place. When one set of solutions has ceased to serve the purpose, another must replace it. Hence, the system ought to be flexible enough to meet the challenge of changing circumstances. It adjusted several times in the past and will change again many more times in the future, given its supporting role in development and new, often unpredictable circumstances. Therefore, the whole transformation should be seen only as a historical episode, albeit a very important one, which may serve development needs well, if policies are managed in an appropriate way.

Contrary to this experience, attention to development policy and treatment of market-oriented reforms as the means for successful development have contributed significantly to the high rate of growth in China and Vietnam (Montes 1997). This is indeed interesting, because there is not yet any such flourishing in terms of durable growth in the postsocialist economies of Eastern Europe and the former Soviet Union. The reforms of the socialist system that failed in Europe still work in Asia. In the latter, it was feasible to distinguish between system design and policy guidance—that is, to take advantage of the system and adjust it as necessary to new challenges for the sake of further growth. This is the ability to use the system and its modification as a means of expansion, and not as a target.

Hence, within each political system there is room for some variation, for distinct policies and exercises. The system itself cannot serve as a substitute for good policy. In history we can see most frequently that it is sufficient to improve policies, without overhauling an entire system. Of course, during transition there is also room for better or worse economic policy, for wise or not-so-wise government action, and for various forms of involvement of the international community.

INSTITUTION BUILDING

We speak of building institutions, but in reality, they must be learned. This is a process. After the failure of "shock therapy" due to the systemic vacuum and deep recession, or better to say depression, the process of postsocialist change has been managed in a more reasonable way, by deliberate measures at a somehow slower pace. By virtue of the very nature of this long-term and complex process, it cannot be carried forward in a radical way. It takes time and is costly in both financial and economic senses. It is risky and can expose a country to social and political tensions. Only part of the multilayer transition process, namely, liberalization linked with stabilization, can be executed—if political conditions permit—in a radical manner. Even this is not an imperative, but a policy choice depending on the scope of monetary and fiscal disequilibria, and on the range of social tolerance.

As for *structural adjustment, institutional reform*, and *behavioral change*, they will take a long time under any conditions. For example, in Eastern Europe it is estimated that about 77 percent of computer software is pirated, while in the United States such malpractice stands at about 20 percent. This is still not insignificant, but four times less common in the United States than in transition economies. Such a difference cannot be explained solely on the basis of more efficient law enforcement and better marketing. The more important difference is that between a weak market culture and a mature one. Yet even in mature markets the process of behavioral change must continue since, despite the sophistication of market institutions and established market culture, as much as one-fifth of computer software is still simply stolen.

Surely, from the viewpoint of the societies concerned and their political elites, it must seem that this will be a lengthy process, but in reality it should be seen as a short historical incident, considering the mighty and comprehensive changes that are taking place. Establishing traditional market economies, although accomplished under different circumstances, took much more time than the current transformations in socialist and postsocialist countries. Ten years is really a short time to turn an economy around. So, the postcommunist transition, despite the hardship it has brought, should be seen as a relatively quick process of complex changes of structures, institutions, and behaviors.

The difficulties have not derived, however, from a lack of knowledge of how the market works, but from difficulty in knowing how to get to a market system from the specific situation of the late socialist economies. The most challenging problem is not finding a target design for new organizations and institutions, but the process of transition leading toward those targets. The most difficult question to be answered, therefore, is not how it should look and work at the very end, but how to get from here to there.

Simultaneously, a process of learning by doing is taking place. Both in the East and West previous theoretical explanations and pragmatic approaches have evolved significantly. Professionals from transition countries have gained knowledge of market performance. Great political and intellectual debates, training at home and abroad, and simple experience of the process have brought tremendous progress vis-à-vis the qualifications of researchers, entrepreneurs, and political elites. Professionals from developed countries, including government representatives dealing with transition, experts from international organizations, and the business community have learned about the specific circumstances of transition. They have been able to absorb information on various features of postsocialist realities, and have understood that one should attack the challenges in a somehow different, rather unorthodox way. Major lessons about the significance of institution building for durable growth have been learned at last, and the proper policy conclusions seem to have been drawn.

Unfortunately, the process of learning by doing has been costly for the Eastern European and post-Soviet nations. To be sure, future growth should not be counted as compensation for the past slump. It was expected and forecasted already several times that production over the whole region will grow, yet in several cases it is not yet a reality. Worse, there are still the postsocialist economies, where output is shrinking and even further contraction, at least in the year 2000, is foreseen (Table

1.2). As for the first ten years of transition, GDP in postsocialist economies contracted more than at the time of the Great Depression in 1929–33. This was not necessary and could have been diminished, if existing knowledge about the possible alternative methods of transformation had not been neglected, and the adjustment of Western economic thought and policy advice to actual challenges had been quicker.

Later, there were better-orchestrated attempts aimed at gradual, but steady institution building. By *institutions* we mean not only organizations and the links between them, but also proper behavior of actors on the economic stage. Thus, with much better coordinated international assistance, transition policies have shifted in a number of countries in the right direction. Market organizations have been created, new laws have been drafted and adopted, and new skills have been taught. Indeed in the late 1990s Eastern Europe, and to a lesser degree the former Soviet Union, look differently than they did in the early 1990s. Yet there is still a long road to travel.

POLICY CONCLUSIONS

It is true that the course of events in postsocialist economies has been under great influence from policies based on the Washington consensus. But it is also true that the transformation to a market economy and occurrences accompanying this process have had significant impact upon the revision of these policies. On the one hand, the line of thought typical for the Washington consensus has had important meaning for the directions of systemic reform and policy attempts in Eastern Europe and the former Soviet Union. On the other hand, the fact that suggested and executed policies did not bring the expected results led to a search for alternative policy means. Actually, the range of issues on which there is consensus among the major partners on the global financial, economic, and political scene has expanded over the years.

The postsocialist transformation has contributed to this evolution of attitudes. New issues and problems have emerged along with the postsocialist markets, and hence there are new concerns, which are far from being agreed on. Nevertheless, there are numerous signs of an urgent need for a new consensus. Additionally several new elements must be emphasized in what has been agreed on in the past. They can be summarized as follows:

1. The main policy conclusion—and the key implication of the post-Washington consensus—is that institutional arrangements are the most

Table 1.2
Forecast of Economic Growth in the Transition Economies, 1998–2002 (data in percentages)

	GDP Index						**Average**	**Ranking**	**GDP index 2002**	
	1997	*Rate of Growth*						*		
	1989 = 100	*1998***	*1999*	*2000*	*2001*	*2002*	*1998–2002*		*1997 = 100*	*1989 = 100*
Poland	111.8	4.8	4.5	5.0	5.4	5.7	5.6	9	128.4	143.2
Slovenia	99.3	4.3	3.7	4.3	4.4	4.8	4.7	15	123.4	122.6
Slovakia	95.6	5.3	2.2	4.0	5.6	6.9	5.3	10	126.3	120.8
Hungary	90.4	5.2	4.3	4.1	4.0	4.1	4.7	13	123.7	111.8
Albania	79.1	4.3	6.2	8.9	8.0	4.4	7.2	4	136.0	107.6
Uzbekistan	86.7	4.5	4.5	4.3	3.8	4.2	4.6	16	123.2	106.8
Czech Republic	95.8	−2.5	0.5	3.3	3.9	5.2	2.1	23	110.6	106.0
Estonia	77.9	6.4	6.1	5.9	6.9	5.9	7.1	5	135.3	105.4
Romania	82.4	−4.7	2.2	4.9	4.8	5.1	2.5	22	112.5	92.7
Croatia	73.3	4.2	2.9	4.3	4.1	4.3	4.3	19	121.4	89.0
Bulgaria	62.8	3.5	2.7	4.6	5.2	5.2	4.6	17	123.0	77.3
Yugoslavia	62.7	5.4	1.3	3.9	4.7	5.5	4.5	18	122.5	76.8
Latvia	56.8	6.6	5.4	4.4	3.9	5.4	5.7	8	128.5	73.0
Kyrgyzstan	58.7	3.0	3.0	4.7	5.2	5.7	4.7	14	123.5	72.5
Turkmenistan	48.3	4.7	12.1	16.0	3.5	4.2	9.4	2	146.8	70.9
Kazakhstan	58.1	1.4	0.6	3.0	5.5	8.3	4.0	20	120.0	69.7
FYR Macedonia	55.3	5.3	4.7	4.6	4.1	4.1	5.0	12	125.0	69.1
Belarus	70.8	4.2	−9.3	−5.8	1.5	2.9	−1.4	26	93.0	65.8

Table 1.2 (*continued*)

	GDP Index						**Average**	**Ranking**	**GDP index 2002**	
	1997	*Rate of Growth*						*		
	1989 = 100	*1998***	*1999*	*2000*	*2001*	*2002*	*1998–2002*		*1997 = 100*	*1989 = 100*
Azerbaijan	40.5	7.9	7.9	9.0	9.9	10.7	10.9	1	154.4	62.5
Lithuania	42.8	7.4	4.5	3.7	3.8	4.1	5.2	11	125.8	53.8
Armenia	41.1	5.7	4.4	5.0	5.7	6.1	6.0	6	129.9	53.4
Tajikistan	40.0	4.3	4.3	5.8	5.5	5.9	5.7	7	128.6	51.4
Russia	52.2	−4.7	−5.3	−2.6	3.9	4.1	−1.0	25	95.1	49.6
Georgia	34.3	7.2	5.1	7.9	9.4	8.0	8.7	3	143.6	49.3
Moldova	35.1	−2.2	0.7	4.1	5.2	6.2	2.9	21	114.5	40.2
Ukraine	38.3	−2.0	−5.2	−1.1	4.0	4.6	0.0	24	100.0	38.3

*Ranking is according to the 2002 GDP index (1997 = 100) and 1998–2002 average rate of growth.
**Author's estimates.

Sources: PlanEcon 1998a and 1998b, and the author's calculations based on Table 1.1.

important factor for progress toward durable growth. What is taken for granted in some market economies (i.e., an institutional setup sufficient for far-going liberalization and free market performance) must be created, often from the outset, in countries moving from statist, centrally planned economies. If there is a choice between developing these institutional arrangements spontaneously (by chance) or in a way directed by the government (by design), then the latter option is more suitable in the case of postsocialist countries. Yet the governments of industrial countries and international organizations must assist several governments in these attempts. Those countries which, due to strong government commitments, were able to take care of such design are doing much better. Recovery has come sooner, growth is robust, and there is the prospect of sustainable development. Those which have tried to trust that major institutional overhaul can occur by itself, by chance, or have not been able to lead this complex process adequately, are lagging behind in both transition advancement and pace of growth.

2. The size of the government is less important than the quality of its policy and how it changes in size. In transition economies the issue is not just downsizing the government, but a deep restructuring of the public finance system and changing the policy targets and means. Basically, fiscal transfers should be redirected from noncompetitive sectors toward institution building (including behavioral and cultural changes), investment in human capital, and hard infrastructure. Attempts to downsize the government through budget cuts can cause more harm than good for launching recovery and growth. Even if a small government is sometimes better than a larger one, the issue is that often it cannot be downsized without causing contraction and standard of living deterioration. Although most often the strongest attempt to downsize is undertaken over a period of deep contraction, in actuality creative downsizing should occur only when the economy is on the rise. Thus, the general problem lies in restructuring expenditures rather than cutting them for an illusion of concurrent, albeit unsustainable fiscal prudence.

3. Unlike certain liberalization measures, institution building by its nature must be a gradual process. Thus feedback between specific "inputs" to this process and its "output" must be monitored constantly and the policies adjusted and corrected as indicated. In postsocialist transition there are many uncharted waters where one should not rely on misguided analogies with experience from distorted market economies. One must consider the specific features of that type of emerging market. Therefore it is necessary to orchestrate some institution building innovation in a

way previously unseen in other places. This is true first regarding privatization and development of capital markets.

4. If institutional arrangement is neglected and left to the spontaneous processes and unleashed forces of liberalized markets, then informal institutionalization fills the systemic vacuum. The negligence of government in organizing market infrastructure with active policy is causing a situation in which informal organizations and institutional links among them are taking over. Extreme cases are vast corruption and organized crime. These are the two main maladies in countries after liberalization and privatization under weak governments. Sometimes governments are too weak because they were forced to become small too early, that is, before the infant market was able to substitute for the state. Prematurely or too extensively downsized government is not strong enough and then the market expands in the informal sector (the shadow economy), while difficulties mount in the official economy. Then profits accrue to the informal sector, but the revenues fall in the official sector, with negative consequences for the budget and social policy. Thus the market works in a way in which profits are privatized, but the losses are socialized in a politically unsustainable way.

5. In transition economies the policies must transform and streamline the judiciary system to serve the needs of a market economy. This is a great challenge, since the old system of contract execution under planned allocation has ceased to exist, but a new system of contract implementation under market rules and culture has not yet matured. The establishment and development of new laws—trade and tax code, capital market regulation, property rights protection, competition and anti-trust rules, banking supervision, consumer protection, environmental protection—are even more important and ought to be addressed before privatization of state assets. Creation and advancement of a legal framework for a market economy should be much higher on the agenda of international financial organizations. It must be put in front, as a more urgent and important issue than liberalization and privatization, since the latter can contribute to sound growth only if the former is secured.

6. A shift of competence and power from the central government to local governments is necessary for deregulation of the postsocialist economy. Such a shift means moving the public finance system toward decentralization, and streamlining local governments by giving them larger fiscal autonomy. Otherwise the process of weakening the central government is not matched by enhancing local governments. The joint position of both levels of government must be seen as an integrated entity

needed for the sake of gradual institution building. If local governments are not enhanced while the central government is weakening, and if market forces are not yet supported by new institutional arrangements, then liberalization and privatization will not necessarily improve capital allocation and will not raise efficiency.

7. There is an urgent need to accelerate the development of NGOs. Next to the private sector and the state, this is the third indispensable pillar of a contemporary market economy and civic society. With a lack of a range of NGOs, which are supposed to take care of various aspects of public life, there is a continued tension between the state and society, and the expanding private sector does not provide sufficient or satisfactory solutions to this matter. There are spheres within the public domain that must depend neither on the state, nor on the profit-oriented private sector. A growing part of international technical, financial, and political assistance must be channeled into enhancing NGOs. Otherwise the infant market economy and democracy in postsocialist countries will not evolve fast enough and the transition will be incomplete. The delay of institutional infrastructure provided by NGOs becomes a growing hurdle for successful systemic changes and high-quality growth.

8. During transition income policy and government concern for equitable growth have great meaning. Whereas increasing inequity is unavoidable during the initial years of transition, the state must play an active role, through fiscal and social policies, in controlling income dispersion. There is a limit of disparity beyond which further expansion of overall economic activity becomes constrained and growth starts to slow or recovery is delayed. If disparity growth is tolerated for a number of years during contraction, when the standard of living is improving for a few and declining for many, then the political support for necessary reforms will evaporate. Hence, large inequities militate against crucial institutional and structural reforms.

9. Postsocialist transition to the market is taking place at a time of worldwide globalization, hence opening and integration with the world economy is an indispensable part of the whole endeavor. Yet these processes must be managed carefully, with special attention to short-term capital flow liberalization. It must be monitored and controlled by the countries' fiscal and monetary authorities with the support of international financial institutions, such as the IMF and BIS. It is better to liberalize capital markets later rather than sooner. First, institution building must be advanced enough, and stabilization ought to be consolidated into stability. Only then should financial markets be liberalized in a grad-

ual manner. Otherwise the societies of young emerging markets and democracies are not going to be supportive of market mechanisms' introduction or integration with the world economy, and they may even become hostile toward such changes.

10. International organizations should not only support, but also insist on further regional integration and cooperation. If growth is expected to be durable and fast, it requires export expansion, which will depend on strong regional links. Thus it calls for institutional support, such as export-import banks, commodity exchanges, credit insurance agencies, and the like. This should be the main institution building concern of the EBRD, supported by directed lending and by technical assistance. This type of market infrastructure is still underdeveloped in transition economies, thus regional trade and cross-country foreign direct investment are lagging behind overall changes. What should be one of the driving forces of sustainable growth, is actually one of its main obstacles.

11. The Bretton Woods organization should reconsider their policies toward transition economies. If the IMF mainly takes care of financial liquidity, currency convertibility, fiscal prudence, and monetary stabilization, the World Bank should focus attention mainly on conditions for equitable growth and sustainable development. For obvious reasons these two kinds of economic policy aims—or rather the means in the former case and the ends in the latter—are often contradictory. There is an inclination to confuse the ends with the means of the policy, to subordinate long-term development policy to short-term stabilization policy. Yet the record of transition so far has clearly proved that there is neither much development nor stability. Hence, in the future fiscal and monetary policies must be subordinated to development policy, not the other way around. There is a need for the World Bank performance criteria describing socioeconomic development as much as there is such a need for traditional IMF fiscal and monetary criteria. The new set of criteria should always stress the implication of advised financial policies for growth, capital allocation, income distribution, and the social safety net. The World Bank should not accept and support policy reforms and actions that, while aiming at financial stabilization, may lead to social destabilization resulting from lack of growth, spreading poverty, increasing inequality, and divestment in human capital.

12. These interactive processes of learning-by-monitoring and learning-by-doing continue and will last for several years. After all, even if there is—as indeed it seems to be—a growing chance for some kind

of the post-Washington consensus, this must be seen as a process, and not as an act. Such an emerging consensus must be accomplished among many more partners than just the important organizations based in Washington. Otherwise, the policies agreed on in Washington will not be able to deliver what they assume elsewhere. This is also an important policy conclusion that should be obvious in the era of globalization. Furthermore, what may be agreed on currently, must be revised often if conditions and challenges change, as they have done recently and undoubtedly will do again and again in the future. Thus the quest for a comprehensive and implementable consensus on policies facilitating sustainable growth must continue.

NOTES

1. From this angle, the Chinese reforms in the late 1990s go along a different line than the earlier Eastern European reforms. China accepts open unemployment, which in 1998 officially exceeded 4 percent (author's estimates).

2. Direct communication between the authors, 1998.

3. This alternative regards policy reorientation executed under the medium-term transition and development program "Strategy for Poland" (Kolodko 1996), when the author was Poland's first deputy prime minister and minister of finance (1994–97). The outline and implementation of this program compared with the earlier policies are described as the Polish Alternative in Kolodko and Nuti (1997).

4. Including those of transition economies.

5. That was a declaration (and unfortunately a way of operating) of the minister of industry and trade of the Polish government at the time of "shock therapy," which as mentioned earlier happened to be shock without therapy.

REFERENCES

Fischer, Stanley. 1998. "Opening Remarks." Presented to the Conference on Economic Policy and Equity. Washington, D.C.: International Monetary Fund. June 8–9.

Fry, Maxwell. 1993. *The Fiscal Abuse of Central Banks*. IMF working paper 93/58. Washington, D.C.: International Monetary Fund.

Hausner, Jerzy. 1997. *The Political Economy of Socialism's Transfor-*

mation. Conference paper. UNU/WIDER Project Meeting: *Transition Strategies, Alternatives and Outcomes*. Helsinki. May 15–17.

IMF. 1996. *Partnership for Sustainable Global Growth*. Interim Committee Declaration. Washington, D.C.: International Monetary Fund. September 29.

Kolodko, Grzegorz W. 1989. *Reform, Stabilization Policies and Economic Adjustment in Poland*. WIDER working papers, no. 51. Helsinki: The United Nations University World Institute for Development Economics Research. January.

———. 1991. "Inflation Stabilization in Poland: A Year After." *Rivista di Politica Economica*, no. 6 (June): 289–330.

———. 1992. *From Output Collapse to Sustainable Growth in Transition Economies—The Fiscal Implications*. Washington, D.C.: International Monetary Fund. December.

———. 1993. "A Strategy for Economic Transformation in Eastern Europe." *Most*, vol. 4, no. 1: 1–25.

———. 1996. *Poland 2000. The New Economic Strategy*. Warsaw: Poltext.

———. 1998. "A Plan for Russia." *The Harriman Review*, Special Issue: *The Russian Economy in Crisis*. Columbia University, New York, December, pp. 24–27.

———. 1999. *From Shock to Therapy. The Political Economy of Postsocialist Transformation*. Oxford: Oxford University Press (forthcoming).

Kolodko, Grzegorz W., and D. Mario Nuti. 1997. *The Polish Alternative. Old Myths, Hard Facts and New Strategies in the Successful Transformation of the Polish Economy*. WIDER Research for Action, no. 33. Helsinki: The United Nations University World Institute for Development Economics Research.

Montes, Manuel. 1997. *Vietnam: Is There a Socialist Road to the Market?* Conference paper. UNU/WIDER Project Meeting: *Transition Strategies, Alternatives and Outcomes*. Helsinki. May 15–17.

North, Douglass C. 1997. *The Contribution of the New Institutional Economics to an Understanding of the Transition Problem*. WIDER annual lectures, no. 1. Helsinki: The United Nations University World Institute for Development Economics Research. March.

Nuti, D. Mario. 1990. "Crisis, Reform and Stabilization in Central Eastern Europe: Prospects and Western Response." In *La Grande Eu-*

ropa, La Nuova Europa: Opportunita e Rischi. Sienna: Monti Dei Paschi Di Sienna. November.

———. 1992. *Lessons from Stabilization and Reform in Central Eastern Europe*. CEC Working Papers, no. 92 (May). Brussels: Council of the European Community.

———. 1996. *Exchange Rate and Monetary Policy in Poland 1994–96, or the Case for Privitising the National Bank of Poland*. Conference paper. UNU/WIDER Project Meeting: *Transition Strategies, Alternatives and Outcomes*. Helsinki. May 15–17.

OECD. 1996. *Czechoslovakia 1996. OECD Economic Surveys*. Paris: Organization for Economic Cooperation and Development.

PlanEcon. 1998a. *Review and Outlook for the Former Soviet Union*. Washington, D.C.: PlanEcon, Inc. October.

———. 1998b. *Review and Outlook for Eastern Europe*. Washington, D.C.: PlanEcon, Inc. December.

Poznanski, Kazimierz. 1993. "Poland's Transition to Capitalism: Shock and Therapy." In *Stabilization and Privatization in Poland*. Ed. K. Poznanski. Boston: Kluwer Academic Publishers.

———. 1996. *Poland's Protracted Transition. Institutional Change and Economic Growth*. Cambridge: Cambridge University Press.

Rosati, Dariusz. 1994. "Output Decline during Transition from Plan to Market." *Economics of Transition*, vol. 2, no. 4: 419–42.

Soros, George. 1997. "The Capitalist Threat." *The Atlantic Monthly*. February.

Stern, Nicholas. 1996. *The Transition in Eastern Europe and the Former Soviet Union: Some Strategic Lessons from the Experience of 25 Countries over Six Years*. Conference paper. OECD/CCET Colloquium. Paris. May. 29–30.

Stern, Nicholas, and Joseph E. Stiglitz. 1997. *A Framework for a Development Strategy in a Market Economy: Objectives, Scope, Institutions and Instruments*. EBRD working paper, no. 20. London: European Bank for Reconstruction and Development. April.

Stiglitz, Joseph E. 1998a. *More Instruments and Broader Goals: Moving Toward the Post-Washington Consensus*. WIDER annual lectures, no. 2. Helsinki: The United Nations University World Institute for Development Economics Research. January.

———. 1998b. *Economic Science, Economic Policy, and Economic Advice*. Conference paper. Annual Bank Conference on Development Economics on *Knowledge for Development*. Washington, D.C.: World Bank. April 20 and 21.

Williamson, John. 1990. "What Washington Means by Policy Reform." In *Latin American Adjustment: How Much Has Happened?* Ed. John Williamson. Washington, D.C.: Institute for International Economics.

———. 1997. "The Washington Consensus Revisited." In *Economic and Social Development into the XXI Century.* Ed. Louis Emmerij. Washington, D.C.: Inter-American Development Bank.

Wolf, Martin. 1998. "Ins and Outs of Capital Flows." *Financial Times,* 16 June.

World Bank. 1996. *From Plan to Market.* World Development Report 1996. Washington, D.C.: World Bank.

———. 1997. *The State in a Changing World. World Development Report 1997.* Washington, D.C.: Oxford University Press for the World Bank.

2

Currency Convertibility in the Transforming Economies

Richard N. Cooper

A striking feature of the economic transformations since 1990 is the rapidity with which former communist countries adopted de facto currency convertibility, at least for current account transactions, and even formally accepted the obligations of Article VIII of the IMF, which calls for convertibility as a basic condition for membership. This stands in marked contrast to the long delay by most OECD countries to make their currencies convertible after the end of the Second World War, and the even longer delay by most developing countries in moving toward currency convertibility. By the spring of 1996 all seven former CMEA countries in Central Europe had currencies that were in practice convertible for current account transactions (with the arguable exception of Romania), and four of those (along with Slovenia, Croatia, and Mongolia) had formally accepted Article VIII. Twelve of the former fifteen republics of the Soviet Union had currencies convertible in practice, and five of those had accepted Article VIII within less than five years of the disintegration of the Soviet Union. In contrast, Western European countries took nearly sixteen years from the end of the war to accept Article VIII (in February 1961), although in practice their currencies had been convertible since 1959; Japan took three years longer, for a total of nearly nineteen years. And in the spring of 1996, well over thirty years after independence and IMF membership, as many as fifty-four developing countries (forty-one in Africa) still maintained exchange controls under the "transitional" IMF

Article XIV—a practice that demonstrated remarkable tolerance, one might even say laxity, by the management of the IMF with respect to the preeminent basic rule of this important financial club.

What explains this huge discrepancy in behavior? Were the former communist countries wise in moving so rapidly (by comparison with others) to current account convertibility? Or in retrospect were the OECD countries and developing countries mistaken to have taken so long? Or were the circumstances so variable that countries were generally correct in taking the different courses they did? Finally, we must at least allow for the logical possibility that the circumstances were different, but that the OECD countries were mistaken in having delayed so long, and the former communist countries were mistaken in moving so quickly.

PROS AND CONS OF CONVERTIBILITY

Full currency convertibility is technically easy to achieve: simply permit everyone, residents and nonresidents alike, to buy and sell home currency for other currencies freely and without restriction. Convertibility for current account transactions (foreign trade in goods and services, including the remittance of earnings), such as is required by the Articles of Agreement of the IMF, is more complicated, since the allowable market is limited to a certain class of transactions—or, put another way, it is designed to exclude certain transactions, especially the purchase by residents of foreign financial assets. It therefore requires some detailed rules and close monitoring, to prevent transactions supposedly made for current purposes from concealing what in fact are capital transactions.[1] When people speak of the difficulty or even the impossibility of a country achieving convertibility, therefore, they must have in mind not convertibility per se, but the economic or political consequences of convertibility.

While convertibility strictly refers to the freedom to purchase foreign exchange for domestic currency, convertibility would not be economically meaningful if licensing were required for the activities that require foreign exchange, such as importing goods or services. In what follows, therefore, I will use *convertibility* in the economically meaningful sense, rather than in the narrowly legal sense, of the term. That is, convertibility cannot be considered independently of the accompanying regime for foreign trade. In particular, a currency is de facto convertible if would-be importers for a wide range of goods or services are free to buy foreign exchange and to import with minimal requirements, possibly subject to import duties that are not prohibitively high.

I will try in the next few paragraphs to sketch the concerns of many policy makers in the early 1950s, and indeed by some in developing countries today, without trying to give historically accurate weights to these concerns. After that, I will sketch some of the advantages alleged for currency convertibility for former communist countries in the 1989–91 period, when their move to market economies was first launched in earnest.

The typical objection to a move to convertibility is that it will lead to an unsustainable loss of foreign exchange reserves and a balance-of-payments crisis. This objection obviously presupposes that the government has pegged the exchange rate, or at least has taken a view on how rapid a change is permissible. If the exchange rate is pegged (including a crawling peg), then an unsustainable outflow of funds, such as through a current account deficit, must be met by some contractionary monetary policy, which in many countries will often imply the need for a smaller government budget deficit. In either case it may lead to a decline in output and income in the short run—something that is never politically popular—and if it persists, it was widely believed, to slower growth in the long run.

The alternative is to alter the rate of exchange between home and foreign currency by enough to stop the outflow—either by allowing it to float, or by depreciating by so much that market participants believe it will depreciate no farther, that imported goods become so expensive in home currency that demand for them will fall significantly, and that exports become so profitable that their supply will increase significantly (or, depending on the significance of our country in the world product market, that the price of exports will fall sufficiently in foreign currency that foreign demand will be greatly stimulated). For a period in the 1950s some "elasticity pessimists" doubted that *any* exchange rate could clear the foreign exchange market, by which they really meant that the required depreciation might be very large. That in turn could have other undesirable consequences, to wit: a sharp increase in the domestic price level, driven by the rise in the prices of tradable goods, which might trigger higher inflationary expectations, either because the public cannot distinguish a once-for-all rise in the price level from an acceleration of inflation, or because the price increase would in fact trigger an inflationary process whereby wage-earners and others attempted to restore their real incomes by insisting on higher nominal wages (and other incomes).

If wage-earners are restrained, the currency depreciation might nonetheless result in a marked deterioration of the distribution of income, especially if the staple food and other key consumption goods are tradable goods, such that their relative prices will rise with currency depreciation. That in turn might lead to serious social and political unrest, even political instability.

These are the kinds of concerns that opponents or skeptics of currency convertibility held in the 1950s, and hold even today in some quarters. In addition, several other inhibitions should be mentioned. First, it might be argued that the practical distinction between current and capital transactions is difficult or impossible to sustain, and that prevention of outflows of resident capital requires controls over current transactions as well, with a view to ensuring domestic savings are invested domestically—for example, as an adjunct of a policy to stimulate economic growth. Second, some governments felt they had a clearer idea than private investors of which activities were required to generate and sustain economic growth, or they took a view of where sectoral growth was especially meritorious. Short of undertaking the desired sectoral investments themselves (as many governments in developing countries did, through state-owned enterprises), they needed some instrument for steering investment in the desired direction. Allocation of credit was the principal chosen instrument in France, Japan, and South Korea, for example, but allocation of foreign exchange played an important adjunct role, and in the early 1950s was perhaps even more important. Even when allocation of foreign exchange was not undertaken aggressively in pursuit of particular objectives, its possible withdrawal was a potent source of discipline over firm managers who were not otherwise inclined to follow the guidance of the planning ministries.

Finally, once exchange controls are in place, there is another, usually unstated, justification for keeping them in place: foreign exchange allocation is a useful channel for political favoritism or personal enrichment, by political leaders and administering officials alike. Especially in poor countries, where control of the government is viewed as one of the few, and perhaps the only sure, route to riches, allocation of foreign exchange under an overvalued currency is one of the ways government authority can be used to enhance tribal, regional, or personal wealth.

Despite this array of concerns with moving to convertibility from a system of tightly rationed foreign exchange, many reform-minded economists accepted the need for a convertible currency as a key component of a market-oriented economy. The question was one of timing. Early reformers in the Soviet Union argued that while convertibility was desirable, it should come, as in postwar Western Europe, late in the process. Thus Abel Aganbegyan, head of the economics section of the Soviet

Academy of Science and adviser to Gorbachev on economic reform, argued that convertibility should be a "long-term objective," to be approached gradually, but he was hardly troubled by the numerous exchange rates applicable to different Soviet industries in the late 1980s and he showed no sense of urgency in establishing convertibility (Aganbegyan 1988, pp. 152, 155). Even the famous five-hundred-day plan of September 1990, urged by academician Shatalin and his reform-minded team and noted for its boldness (which led Gorbachev to back away from it), foresaw convertibility coming late in the reforms, possibly years after the five-hundred-day initial push. And reformer (and former finance minister) Boris Fedorov wrote in late 1990 of current account convertibility as "a medium-term target" (Fedorov in Williamson 1991, p. 290).

Others thought that currency convertibility should be an integral part of a program of economic transformation from a centrally planned to a market economy, to be introduced early in the program, with price liberalization. One illustration is to quote the argument put in an International Institute for Applied System Analysis (IIASA) report transmitted in the mid-1990s to Soviet Deputy Prime Minister (for economic policy) Abalkin and to the Shatalin team (Cooper in Peck, Aven, and Richardson 1991, pp. 117–18; see also McKinnon [1991], Sachs [1993], and Balcerowicz [1995]).

> There are several reasons for preferring that the opening of the economy occur early rather than late. First, the key to a modern, flexible and innovative economy is competitive markets, wherein information on new patterns of demand or new technological developments is transmitted to the entire economy through price signals, to which both households and enterprises can respond by adapting their behavior. The Soviet Union has intentionally concentrated production of most manufactured goods in one or relatively few enterprises. Monopolies do not respond to market signals in the same way as other enterprises, and their responses are not socially optimal. Some method must be found for introducing competitive pressures on Soviet enterprises at an early stage of restructuring so that enterprises feel these pressures in making their decisions. One way to do this, and for some sectors the only effective way, is to introduce foreign competition, so that Soviet enterprises have a price and a quality standard that they must match in order to sell at home or abroad.
>
> A second reason for introducing currency convertibility early is

> to encourage from the beginning an alignment of Soviet prices with world prices of traded goods and services, subject to such deviations as the economic authorities wish explicitly and consciously to make. If, as we assume, this alignment with world prices is the final objective, then starting the process early would be more advantageous than going through a domestic price liberalization and then having a second major price realignment when the economy is opened. The alternative of administrative price adjustment to approximate world prices is inadvisable, both because it perpetuates the principle of administrative control of prices (as opposed to market determined prices) and because such control cannot be fully effective in a world with millions of products of diverse qualities.
>
> A third reason for favoring early convertibility of the ruble is to provide goods to Soviet workers whose incentive to work is now adversely affected by extensive shortages. Opening the economy would offer a wide array of new goods, albeit for purchase at high prices. It would not only provide effective wage goods, but would also help reduce the ruble overhang, since firms and households would be more willing to hold financial assets, which are not high by western standards. It would also provide the Government with revenue from taxes levied on imports, as we propose below.
>
> Finally, convertibility would provide a strong stimulus to develop export markets. At the exchange rate required to make the ruble convertible, exports would be extremely profitable for newly independent enterprises. Autonomous enterprises would have a strong financial incentive to develop export markets, and that would push them from the beginning to take into account not only the price but also the quality of products that are sold in the world market.

While the argument was made for the then Soviet Union, it has more general applicability to the shift of any command economy to a market-oriented one. And in fact currency convertibility was introduced in the early reform packages of many of them, or soon thereafter. We will explore below the extent to which the concerns expressed by those anxious about currency convertibility came to pass. We will turn first to a discussion of some of the considerations inhibiting a move toward convertibility in Europe in the late 1940s and early 1950s. The experience of the Western European countries is an interesting case to be analyzed given the strong economic development of the region in the following decades.

EUROPEAN CONVERTIBILITY IN THE LATE 1940s

Early acceptance of IMF Article VIII was inhibited by several factors in the late 1940s. Britain, while diminished, was still the key industrial economy of Europe, especially as a trading nation at the economic and financial center of the Sterling Area, which comprised most of what is now the British Commonwealth plus several other countries. The key to Europe was thus Britain. But Britain was reluctant to move to convertibility for a variety of mutually reinforcing reasons.

First, sterling balances around the world, especially in Africa and India, were still large, and (external) convertibility would have permitted the holders of sterling to import from anywhere, straining Britain's reserves.

Second, the short-lived July 1947 experiment in convertibility, a condition of the 1946 Anglo-American loan, had led to an intolerable loss of reserves.

Third, Britain's reconstruction (and new housing construction) needs were still being met, so Britain had little productive capacity for additional exports (an argument that was applied elsewhere in Europe).

Fourth, there was a "dollar shortage," that is, a tendency for the United States to export more than it imported; correcting this with currency devaluation was thought by some to be of dubious value, because U.S. demand was allegedly price-inelastic and in any case European exports were supply-constrained, as in the third point.

Fifth, convertibility on current account was incompatible with the price controls that still prevailed in Britain and elsewhere (except Germany after mid-1948), and these in turn were an essential component of the Labour Party's program (Britain's Chancellor of Exchequer Sir Stafford Cripps denounced advice to devalue the pound on the (correct) grounds that it favored a "free economy"—quoted in James 1996, p. 95).

These arguments were generally accepted, in whole or in part, by many contemporaries. Diebold's (1952) classic study of European trade and payments focuses largely on the struggle to overcome bilateralism, and does not even discuss the possibility of a general move to currency convertibility. Kindleberger (1950) expounded on the existence and permanence of a dollar shortage. Triffin (1957 and 1966, collecting his memos and papers of the late 1940s and early 1950s) focuses on the need for monetary stability and accepts fixed exchange rates in that context. Only Friedman (1953, memo written in late 1950) argues the case for flexible exchange rates and convertible currencies, a view that was considered idiosyncratic and even quixotic at the time.[2] The practical problem was seen to be the restraints on growth implied by the bilateral trade restrictions prevalent in the late 1940s. The solution was to create the European Payments Union (EPU) in 1950, which provided for a limited but gradually increasing current account convertibility among the Western European currencies (and the Sterling Area, encompassing Australia, India, Pakistan, New Zealand, and Britain's still extensive colonial empire).

After the large 1949 devaluations and the 1951 election that returned the Tories to power in Britain and brought price liberalization, some British officials were much more sympathetic to convertibility, if necessary even floating the pound to achieve it (James 1996, pp. 99–101; Kaplan and Schleiminger, 1989, pp. 160–66). Canada had floated its dollar during the Korean War commodity boom in 1950. But Britain was still concerned about the sterling balance and a dollar shortage and wanted to continue to discriminate against dollar goods (e.g., through invocation of IMF Article VII).

Eichengreen (1993) examines the possibility that European currencies could have been made current account convertible in 1950, in lieu of establishing EPU. He examines four of Janos Kornai's five criteria for convertibility (pp. 43–44): a realistic exchange rate consistent with payments equilibrium, sufficient foreign exchange reserves, absence of a monetary overhang, and adequate wage discipline (Kornai's fifth criterion, that firms face hard budget constraints, was judged not relevant to Western Europe in 1950). Using a series of relatively simple quantitative tests, Eichengreen concludes that modest devaluation after the 1949 devaluations would have met the first criterion; the second was attained by 1950 (at least compared to the late 1920s); the third did not apply after 1950 except (significantly) to Britain and Ireland, due in part to sterling balances; and wage restraint was maintained adequately during the 1950s. However, Eichengreen argues that wage restraint might not have obtained in the absence of the EPU, and therefore cannot be taken for granted under the counterfactual alternative of currency convertibility.

The basic argument is as follows: Europe after the First World War had cut itself up economically and politically over the distribution of income. Political leaders wished to avoid this after the Second World War. The "postwar settlement" involved an exchange of wage restraint by labor for a commitment by business (or government, through corporate taxes) to reinvest business earnings rather than distribute them to owners of capital, with a view to raising productivity and economic growth, and hence ultimately also real wages (but not the wage share). Many devices were introduced to this end. The Marshall Plan helped facilitate this implicit bargain by permitting some investment that was not financed out of household income or retained earnings. The EPU permitted more favorable terms of trade for Europe, by discriminating against dollar goods, than would have been possible under currency convertibility, amounting to 1 to 2 percent of GDP (Eichengreen 1993, p. 86). This amount, by permitting larger-than-otherwise consumption or investment, may have been enough to ensure wage restraint.

There was also a coordination problem. While Eichengreen shows that currency convertibility could have worked overall, any individual country might have found itself with a dollar deficit matched by an (inconvertible) surplus against other countries. Thus a coordinated move to convertibility was required. The EPU ultimately permitted this, although other mechanisms no doubt could have been found.

This argument is ingenious and appealing (Eichengreen also ties it to the need to revive the German economy). But the weakness is the United Kingdom. If, as Eichengreen concedes, Britain had an unacceptably large monetary overhang until 1955, and if, as suggested above, Britain was the key to European equilibrium, then convertibility would not have been possible until after 1955 without funding the sterling balances (as many contemporaries urged) or tolerating a further once-for-all rise in British prices, followed by another devaluation. But convertibility was well advanced by the mid-1950s and might have been achieved in 1956 had it not been for the financial setback created by the Suez crisis.

I will not explore for Western Europe in the 1950s the performance criteria discussed for Eastern Europe in the 1990s. Suffice it to say that economic growth during the 1950s was generally above 3 percent a year (2.8 for Britain, lowest among the major countries); inflation was generally 2 to 3 percent a year, except in France, where average annual inflation of 5.6 percent reduced the value of money by 42 percent over the decade; and the volume of export growth, both permitting and encouraged by liberalization of trade and payments, was 7 to 15 percent a year, except for Britain's paltry 1.7 percent.[3]

TRADE AND PAYMENTS LIBERALIZATION IN EASTERN EUROPE

By 1994 all the former communist countries of Eastern Europe (as well as the three Baltic states) were rated by the EBRD to have earned

Table 2.1
Trade and Exchange Rate Practices (1994 average)

	Liberalization Introduced/Time	Exchange Rate Regime	Accepted Article VIII	Import Tariff (in %)	Import Tariff Range in 1994
Bulgaria	3/91; 7/91 . . .	Float	n.a.	17	5–55
Czech Republic	1/91	Fixed	10/95	5	0–80
Hungary	12/90 . . .	Managed	1/96	15	5–83
Poland	1/90	Managed	6/95	13	0–43
Romania	1/91, 1/92, 5/92 . . .	Float	n.a.	12	0–60
Slovak Republic	1/91	Fixed	10/95	2	0–25
Slovenia	2/92	Managed	9/95	11	0–25
Estonia	6/92	Fixed	8/94	< 10	0–16
Latvia	5/92	Managed	6/94	< 15	0–55
Lithuania	6/92 . . .	Fixed	5/94	10	0–30

Sources: IMF, *Annual Report on Exchange Arrangements and Exchange Restrictions*, various years; *International Financial Statistics*, April 1996.

the highest mark under the heading of price and trade liberalization, on a scale of 1 to 4. But both the timing and the speed of liberalization varied substantially from country to country. Hungary and Poland began price liberalization in the 1980s (Slovenia, then part of Yugoslavia, began even earlier). But Poland experienced the "big bang," encompassing full price and payments liberalization as well as a major stabilization program in January 1990. Hungary took important steps during 1990, but continued to liberalize more gradually, particularly regarding the allocation of foreign exchange. Czechoslovakia introduced its own version of the big bang in January 1991, but that did not need to be so radical as Poland in terms of stabilizing actions, and it was modestly less radical in freeing the allocation of foreign exchange (see Table 2.1).

Albania, Bulgaria, and Romania took a series of liberalizing steps during 1991 and 1992, which in the latter two cases carried them less far than Poland and Czechoslovakia, but left them all with currencies that were in practice convertible for most current transactions. Slovenia separated from Yugoslavia in 1992 and introduced its own currency; the Baltic states separated their currencies and economic systems from Russia in May and June of the same year, all three introducing radical and abrupt liberalization, although the details differed (e.g., Estonia fixed its new currency with respect to the German mark, whereas the new currencies of Latvia and Lithuania were allowed to float until 1994). Poland, Hungary, Czechoslovakia, and Estonia began with fixed (albeit depreciated) exchange rates. Albania, Bulgaria, Romania, Slovenia, Latvia, and Lithuania initially adopted flexible exchange rates, although in 1994 the last two switched to fixed rates (Lithuania formally, Latvia in practice) as they managed to bring inflation under control. Hungary continued to depreciate the florint from time to time, adopting a formal crawling peg in 1995, and Poland also adopted a managed float/crawling peg once the stabilization had taken hold. By 1995 Slovenia had also adopted a managed float, that is, the authorities intervened regularly in the foreign exchange market to influence movement of the exchange rate.

Countries also simplified and generally lowered their tariffs and eliminated import quotas and requirements for import licensing at around the same time they introduced convertible currencies (the Baltics introduced new tariff systems at generally low rates). In most cases these early tariff systems were refined and raised somewhat (particularly the maximum rates) as time went on, but remained low (i.e., averaging 5 to 17 percent) by the standards of most developing countries. Estonia and Lithuania began at virtually free trade, but then imposed revenue tariffs.

As noted at the outset, these changes were much more abrupt than the liberalization of trade and payments introduced by Western European countries in the 1950s and by most developing countries over the 1980s and 1990s. How are we to assess their relative success? We look at five measures: economic growth, consumption, export performance, inflation, and capital flows.

Economic Growth. One standard is to look at what happened to total economic output (GDP, or an approximation thereof). Output declined in all Eastern European countries relative to 1989 (see Table 2.2). By 1994 output was growing in all of these countries, although it continued to fall in some other republics from the former Soviet Union (Fischer, Sahay, and Vegh 1996, Table 2). Even though reforms began in 1990 or 1991 for most of the countries (except the Baltics), output reached its bottom in 1993 for all except Poland (1991), Romania (1992), and Slovenia (1992). Recovery resumed more quickly, in other words, in Poland and the Baltics, countries that liberalized relatively quickly, than in gradualist Bulgaria and Hungary. However, quick liberalizer Czechoslovakia also experienced economic decline for three years.

Total output, however, is suspect as a measure of success in these reforming economies. First, total output is poorly measured, particularly

Table 2.2
Performance Indexes, 1995 (1990 = 100)

	Output	Real Household Consumption	Exports (U.S.$)	Consumer Prices	Real Monthly Wages
Bulgaria	74	87	82	4267	45
Czech Republic	81	95	228	253	98
Hungary	83	93[a]	103	381[a]	88[a]
Poland	93	108[a]	133	3922[a]	71[a]
Romania	77	79	109	6578	97
Slovak Republic	78	75	248	272	84
Slovenia	89	n.a.	190	1172	107
Estonia	67	n.a.	404[b]	361[b]	n.a.
Latvia	49	39[c]	143[b]	355[b]	119[b]
Lithuania	40	n.a.	1075[b]	1225[b]	75[b]

[a]1989 = 100.
[b]1992 = 100.
[c]1993.

Sources: Col. 1, Fischer et al. (1996); col. 2, OECD (April 1995); cols. 3–5, *International Financial Statistics*, WEFA (1996), and WIIW (1995).

in the early years of reform; new economic activity permitted or encouraged by the liberalization is greatly undercounted, due to inadequacies in statistical collection. Second, and more important, much of the output in the former communist countries was socially without value (although it used resources), so substantial reductions in output by the existing enterprises was warranted and indeed (although rarely acknowledged by officials) in my judgment was actually desirable.

Real Consumption. A more appropriate measure of the impact of liberalization involves looking at real consumption.[4] Column 2 of Table 2.2 shows an estimate of the cumulative decline in real consumption between the year preceding major liberalization (1989 for Hungary and Poland, 1990 or 1991 for others) and 1995. The change ranges from an increase of 8 percent in Poland to a decline of 25 percent in Slovakia (and, for comparison, of 34 percent in Russia; consumption data for the three Baltics are not available). This measure does not permit a clear award between rapid and gradual liberalization, since Slovakia was originally in the rapid category; but the favorable experience of Poland relative to Hungary and the Czech Republic against Bulgaria and Romania suggests that rapid liberalization is not necessarily more costly. Consumption can be sustained and even increased if a country runs a growing current account deficit. Among these countries there is little marked trend in current account positions during the 1990s; if anything, there is a modest tendency toward declining deficits or larger surpluses. The notable exception is Hungary, which ran substantial deficits in 1993 and 1994, although the deficit declined after the adoption of an austerity program and small devaluation in the spring of 1995.

Export Performance. A third possible standard of success would be export performance. Much work following Little, Scitovsky, and Scott (1970) and Balassa (1971) has suggested that one of the most insidious—and growth-inhibiting—consequences of heavy restrictions on imports is their discouragement of exports, through several channels but especially the exchange rate. To the extent this argument is correct, liberalization of imports should encourage exports, and in general the faster the better. Column 3 of Table 2.2 shows the annualized percentage increase in dollar value of exports from the year before the major year of reform (the year of the reform in the case of the Baltics) to 1995. There it can be seen that the relative gradualists among these countries—Bulgaria, Hungary, and Romania—also experienced the slowest growth in exports; indeed exports from Bulgaria actually declined.

Several comments should be made about the export environment. First, countries varied in their trade dependence with other members of the CMEA, ranging from 3 percent of GDP for Romania to 16 percent for Poland in 1990. And of course the Baltics traded heavily within the former Soviet Union (ranging from 27 to 34 percent of 1990 GDP) and Slovenia within the former Yugoslavia.[5] The rapid growth of exports may be explained in part by the diversion of products from formerly internal trade to new export markets.

Second, the overall economic performance of the major export market for all these countries, the EU, was mediocre in 1991 and 1992, after rapid growth in 1989–90; final demand of the EU actually declined by nearly 2 percent in 1993, followed by modest recovery in 1994 and 1995.

Third, export growth is dependent on competitiveness, and especially for manufactured goods that depends in some measure on labor costs, measured in foreign currency, as well as on quality, packaging, and a host of other factors. A move to currency convertibility accompanied by currency depreciation to ration limited supplies of foreign exchange will lower wages measured in foreign currency, unless labor successfully bargains for a proportionate increase in wages. The extent of the liberali-

Table 2.3
Monthly Manufacturing Wages (in U.S. dollars)

	1989	1990	1991	1992	1993	1994	1995[a]
Bulgaria[b]		137	64	97	120	113	122
Czech Republic		190	133	162	196	231	303
Hungary	154	170	185	224	237	249	249
Poland	149	105	158	168	175	191[a]	290[c]
Romania	168	123	100	61	74	80	101
Slovak Republic				161	175	196	239
Slovenia				628	666	735	968
Estonia				44	78	137	219
Latvia				32	79	142	198
Lithuania					47	84	136
United States		1496	1534	1576	1619	1674	1694

[a]Second quarter.
[b]Public sector.
[c]Gross wage.

Sources: Calculated from OECD (April 1995); *International Financial Statistics*; Bosworth and Gur (1995), p. 131.

zation in general will influence the extent of the required depreciation, and that in turn will influence wage costs measured in foreign currency. Table 2.3 sets out monthly wages in manufacturing in these countries, converted into dollars at the prevailing exchange rate. An inspection of the rows shows that wages in dollars generally dropped in years of major liberalization, the notable exception being Hungary, where liberalization was stretched over several years. Wages dropped by 30 percent in Poland in 1990, and by a similar amount in the Czech Republic in 1991. They dropped by over 50 percent in Bulgaria in 1991, and by a similar amount in Romania over the 1991–92 period. From these low points wages in dollars grew, often rapidly, as domestic wage increases exceeded the rate of currency depreciation. This is a pattern that one would expect, indeed welcome, as new export markets are established and developed.

Inspection of Table 2.3 offers a direct comparison of manufacturing wages across the different countries. The sometimes striking differences reflect variations in productivity, as well as the different extent and timing of trade liberalization and currency depreciation. It is noteworthy that monthly manufacturing wages in the former Soviet Union, other than the Baltics, were all under $25 in 1992, and remained under $100 (except for Kazakhstan) in 1995, reflecting the strong depreciation of the ruble and its successor currencies in the other republics.

Inflation. To the extent convertibility requires substantial depreciation, the authorities may be concerned with triggering or aggravating inflationary expectations. One manifestation might be greater capital outflows, discussed immediately below. Actual inflation did indeed rise substantially in all the East European countries, relative to the suppressed inflation prior to liberalization. Column 4 of Table 2.2 shows the consumer price level in 1995 relative to pre-reform levels. The figures show that Hungary, a gradualist, performed much better on this measure than did Poland, which moved rapidly. But the Czech Republic and Slovakia also moved quickly, and they performed better than Hungary. And Bulgaria and Romania, both gradualists among these countries, experienced markedly higher rates of inflation than the other countries. Among the Baltics, Estonia, which moved rapidly, ultimately experienced less increase in prices than did Lithuania, which liberalized more slowly. Of course, movements in prices of these magnitudes reflect largely the degree of control over closely related fiscal and monetary policies, the lower inflation countries having maintained much more effective monetary control. Thus the observed inflation can be attributed only in small part to the liberalization. But the *ex post* data offer little comfort to those who favor gradualism.

Capital Outflows. Another indirect measure of the acceptability of the liberalization of foreign exchange transactions, necessarily with extensive depreciation, and of higher uncompensated inflationary expectations, is the extent to which capital left the country, despite widespread formal controls on international capital outflows. While private capital left various countries from time to time, the balance-of-payments statistics (including errors and omissions) reveal no major recorded or unrecorded outflows of private capital from East European countries, in sharp contrast to both China and Russia, for instance, where for quite different reasons substantial outflows have occurred. Of course, there still may have been substantial outflows concealed by roughly equivalent inflows that also were not recorded, such as underreporting of exports offset by increased investment abroad, including in foreign currency. Both Poland and Czechoslovakia ran substantial but transitory current account surpluses in the year of their major reforms, due in part to the sharp price-induced decline in real incomes in those years.

It is difficult on these measures to distinguish sharply between those countries that liberalized quickly and those that did so more gradually, although as noted those that liberalized quickly seemed to have, on balance, slightly better performance on the indicators discussed. Extending the sample to include other formerly communist countries, especially the republics of the former Soviet Union, offers one possibility for sorting out the influence of liberalization, since the extent of liberalization is much more varied if those countries are included.

Such an exercise has been carried out by Anders Åslund and his colleagues (1996, Table 3). They regress cumulative output decline through 1995 against a "liberalization index" for each of twenty-four former communist countries in 1994, taken from the World Bank (de Melo, Denzier, and Gelb, 1996). (Unfortunately for our purposes, the liberalization index goes beyond price, foreign exchange, and foreign trade liberalization to include private-sector entry and other factors.) The regression suggests that cumulative liberalization mitigated the decline in output significantly, countries that liberalized less having experienced, on average, a sharper decline in output. However, closer inspection of the data suggests that the steepest declines in output occurred in former republics of the Soviet Union; if dummies are inserted for membership in the ruble zone or for being riven by war (Armenia, Azerbaijan, Croatia, Georgia, Macedonia, Tajikistan), the significance of the liberalization variable disappears. A similar result obtains for unemployment (ibid., Table 8). While the demise of CMEA in 1991 was no doubt a serious short-term economic disturbance to Eastern European countries, the disintegration of the Soviet Union was an even greater disturbance to its constituent members, whose economies were closely linked through decades of Moscow-directed central planning, with its emphasis on economies of scale and monopoly production, especially in manufacturing.

Farther afield, output fell between 1989 and 1994 by about a third in both Cuba and North Korea, two completely unreformed communist systems heavily dependent on the former Soviet Union for trade and aid. Too many things were happening at the same time to sort out persuasively the impact of trade and payments liberalization.

It is noteworthy, however, that cumulative liberalization does help to explain economic growth in 1995, and the explanatory power is only slightly diminished by including dummies for membership in the ruble area and being war-torn (Åslund et al. 1996, Table 5), suggesting that early and more extensive liberalization yields earlier and stronger returns in terms of output. Moreover, the effect is even stronger than revealed if, as is likely, unrecorded output growth in new economic activity is higher in the countries that have liberalized more extensively.

Income Distribution. One of the concerns about currency convertibility in postwar Western Europe involved the distribution of income. A move to convertibility, accompanied either by reductions in output or by currency depreciation, was thought to fall especially heavily on the low-wage worker, since Europe at the time was still heavily dependent on food imports, whose domestic price could be expected to rise with currency devaluation. Table 2.3 measures Eastern European wages in dollars in the early 1990s. But the figures there also offer some indication of what has happened to real wages in the transforming economies, and indirectly something about the distribution of income. We have already seen that consumption fell substantially below income; much pre-reform production was destined for the military services and investment in the defense-supporting industries. Cutting such production would not directly affect the distribution of income, except insofar as workers employed in those industries found themselves moving from high- to low-wage activity, or from employment to uncompensated unemployment. This change would arise from changes in the structure or level of output. The distinctive contribution to changes in the distribution of income arising from trade and payments liberalization would arise from changes in relative consumer-good prices that arise, directly or indirectly, from such liberalization. The most obvious example would be a liberalization-induced rise in the prices of staple foods, especially grain. On the other hand, the relative price of housing, still under price control in most reforming countries, and in any case experiencing extensive inertia, should fall in the face of liberalization-induced increases in commodity prices, and the share of housing in household budgets may be expected to fall as money wages increase in even partial response to the rise in commodity prices.

Column 5 of Table 2.2 shows the real monthly wage in manufacturing in 1995 relative to 1990 (1989 for Poland and Hungary, 1992 for the Baltics), where the real wage has been calculated using the consumer price index. The change ranges from increases of 19 percent in Latvia and 7 percent in Slovenia to declines of 55 percent in Bulgaria and 29 percent in Poland (all of the Polish decline occurred in 1990, wages having kept up with prices thereafter). There is no obvious pattern according to the pace of liberalization. Hungary preserved the real wage much better than Poland (although the positions would be reversed if

1990 was used as the year of comparison), a fast liberalizer, but not significantly better than the Czech Republic, also a fast liberalizer, which preserved real wages much better than gradualists Romania and especially Bulgaria. Wage data are in any case incomplete, particularly in view of a sharp increase in activity in the service sectors, much of it informal. For example, a comparison of household consumption (column 2) with real wages (column 5) for Hungary and Poland raises serious questions about one or both sets of data—or points to an exceptional increase in nonwage income in Poland.

A careful study of income distribution in the Baltic states in 1994 compared with 1990, based on household survey data, suggests a considerable increase in dispersion of income in all three countries, with the Gini coefficient rising from 0.24 by 0.10 in Estonia, 0.11 in Lithuania, and 0.17 in Latvia, with some caveats for lack of complete comparability between the 1990 and the 1994 data (Cornelius and Weder 1996, Tables 1 and 2). More comprehensibly, the ratio of income in the top decile of the surveyed population to that in the bottom decile, a common rough measure of income inequality, rose from around 3.2 in 1990 in all three Baltics to 5.0 in Estonia, 6.6 in Lithuania, and 8.9 in Latvia in 1994. Most of these increases came about because of increased wage dispersion, wages accounting for one-half to two-thirds of household income, and most of that in turn came mainly from relative reductions in wages at the low end of the wage scale rather than increases at the high end, at least in terms of reported income.

These figures, however interesting, do not establish the relevance of trade and payments liberalization on income distribution, since the analysis concerns money income, without regard to the pattern of household expenditure and changes in the pattern of relative prices. At the times of liberalization, most Hungarian domestic prices were already free from control, as were Polish food prices. Bulgaria and Czechoslovakia, however, maintained a full set of price controls (Bosworth and Ofer 1995, p. 120). A detailed study is required of the postliberalization rise or fall in relative prices plausibly attributable to liberalization of international trade and payments, and a comparison of these relative price effects with expenditure patterns by household income class, before and after liberalization. (For example, the relative prices of household appliances presumably declined with liberalization, and product quality greatly improved.)

FIFTIES VERSUS NINETIES: WHAT EXPLAINS THE DIFFERENCE?

It is useful to recall the climate of opinion that prevailed in Western Europe in the late 1940s, and to contrast it with Western Europe in the late 1980s, for substantial differences therein go some way toward explaining the divergent approaches to convertibility. The world had just emerged in the late 1940s from the Great Depression of the 1930s and a devastating war that had its origins in part in the social hardship of that Depression. One legacy of that experience was high sensitivity to unemployment. Moreover, the Great Depression at a minimum had raised questions about the stability and long-run viability of a capitalist, free market economic system, and had persuaded many that government must play a much greater role in economic management—not only in sustaining aggregate demand, the main lesson of the Keynesian revolution in economic thinking, but also in directing investment and more generally in "planning" the evolution of the structure of output and even patterns of consumption.

A second legacy was a strong distaste for floating exchange rates, associated with the turbulent and disorderly periods immediately following the First World War and again in the early 1930s, as documented and interpreted by Nurkse (1944).

A third legacy from the interwar period was the presence in most Western European countries of sharp ideological cleavages reflected in political parties, at least along Marxist/anti-Marxist lines, but often also accompanied by cross-cutting cleavages along religious or monarchist/republican lines. Britain, France, and Italy, in particular, were all plagued by bitter ideological differences among leading members of the political community.

Eastern European countries by the late 1980s, in contrast, had experienced forty years of full employment and enforced ideological uniformity in the body politics, which was all but universally rejected as having been imposed from outside. There was wide public consensus in most countries on the desirability of breaking sharply with the recent past and moving toward greater economic (as well as political) freedom. This was understood to mean shedding the system of central planning in favor of a market-oriented allocation of resources, and this in turn implied a radical change in the composition of output. Controls over the allocation of foreign exchange were associated with the general system of centralized controls under communist rule, as well as with corruption by officials, and as such were to be rejected as heinous. Moreover, the previous unavailability of many foreign goods, especially processed foods and household durables, meant that availability even if at high prices represented an improvement, and a decline in measured real wages would not be indicative of a parallel decline in the sense of material well-being.

In addition, the major foreign currencies had been floating against one another for nearly twenty years, since 1973, with attendant inconvenience but without obvious disaster or strong negative associations.

These differences do not represent arguments why currency convertibility would have been more successful in one period than in another. Rather, they suggest why a rapid move to currency convertibility was more acceptable politically in Eastern Europe in the 1990s than it would have been in Western Europe in the 1950s. Insofar as temporarily higher unemployment can be associated with a rapid move to currency convertibility (which is not in fact established by the recent record of Eastern Europe, but cannot be ruled out either), the approaches reflect different antecedent conditions and social values based on those antecedent conditions. West Europeans (especially the British) inherited economic controls established during a major war they had just won, and they were intrigued by the possibility that peacetime controls might reduce or eliminate the manifest instability of a capitalist economy; East Europeans inherited economic controls from a largely externally imposed political regime which they wished to shed as quickly and as completely as possible.

CONCLUSION

Few hard conclusions can be drawn from this examination, and those that can are largely negative. First, a rapid move to currency convertibility (on current account) by the transforming countries of Eastern Europe does not seem to have hurt those countries that undertook it compared with those that moved more gradually, on the usual criteria for economic improvement; indeed, on balance they seem to have performed better, but the evidence is not conclusive and in particular the number of observations is too few (even when augmented by the former republics of the Soviet Union) to make strong conclusions after allowance is made for other differentiating features among countries.

Second, Western European countries almost surely could have moved to currency convertibility more rapidly than they did in the 1950s, especially if arrangements had been made for partial funding of the sterling balances held by Commonwealth countries, but the intellectual climate and political consensus were not present for making the move or for absorbing such short-run turbulence as may have followed a move to convertibility.

Third, the experience of the Eastern European countries in the early 1990s, although admittedly embedded in special circumstances, at least raises strong doubts about the justification for preserving exchange controls in many developing countries—a much heavier burden of proof should be levied on those countries by the international community and in particular by the IMF, whose Articles of Agreement call for currency account convertibility as a basic condition for membership in the Fund.

NOTES

1. For example, it may be expedient to limit the amount of foreign currency a resident can buy for the purpose of foreign travel—a current transaction—to prevent the export of capital for purchase of assets abroad. Travel arranged and prepaid through a monitored travel agency would be unrestricted.

2. Triffin (1966, pp. 180–94, internal IMF memos written in 1949) argues that in the interests of trade liberalization the IMF should encourage member countries to adopt flexible exchange rates, under IMF surveillance, as a strictly transitory measure.

3. Author's estimates.

4. In most of these countries total real consumption tracks per capita consumption closely since, remarkably, population in all the countries is growing slowly or, in a few cases, declining slowly.

5. Data are from Fischer, Sahay, and Vegh (1996), Table 1.

REFERENCES

Aganbegyan, Abel. *The Economic Challenge of Perestroika*. Bloomington: University of Indiana Press, 1988.

Åslund, Anders. *How Russia Became a Market Economy*. Washington, D.C.: Brookings Institution, 1995.

Åslund, Anders, Peter Boone, and Simon Johnson. *How to Stabilize: Lessons from Post-Communist Countries*. Brookings Papers on Economic Activity, no. 1, 1996.

Balassa, Bela. *The Structure of Protection in Developing Countries*. Baltimore: Johns Hopkins University Press for the International Bank for Reconstruction and Development, 1971.

Balcerowicz, Leszek. *Socialism, Capitalism, Transformation*. Budapest: Central European University Press, 1995.

Bosworth, Barry P., and Gur Ofer. *Reforming Planned Economies in an Integrating World Economy* Washington, D.C.: Brookings Institution, 1995.

Cooper, Richard N. "Currency Convertibility in Eastern Europe." In *Central Banking Issues in Emerging Market Economies*. Federal Bank of Kansas City, 1990.

———. "Opening the Soviet Economy." In *What Is to Be Done? Proposals for the Soviet Transition to Market*. Ed. M. J. Peck, Petr Aven, and Thomas Richardson. New Haven: Yale University Press, 1991.

Cornelius, Peter K., and Beatrice S. Weder. *Economic Transformation and Income Distribution: Some Evidence from the Baltic Countries*. IMF working paper, WP/96/14, February 1996.

de Melo, Martha, Cerdet Denzier, and Alan Gelb. *From Plan to Market: Partners of Transition*. Policy Research Department Working Paper, 1564, World Bank, Washington, D.C., 1996.

Diebold, William. *Trade and Payments in Western Europe: A Study in Economic Cooperation, 1947–51*. New York: Harper & Row, 1952.

Economist Intelligence Unit. *Country Report* for various countries. London: EIU, 1996.

Eichengreen, Barry. *Reconstructing Europe's Trade and Payments: The European Payments Union*. Manchester: Manchester University Press, 1993.

Federal Reserve Bank of Kansas City. *Central Banking Issues in Emerging Market Economies*. Kansas City: Federal Reserve Bank, 1990.

Fischer, Stanley, Ratna Sahay, and Carlos A. Vegh. "Stabilization and Growth in Transition Economies: The Early Experience." IMF working paper, March 1996.

Friedman, Milton. "The Case for Flexible Exchange Rates." In *Essays in Positive Economics*. Chicago: University of Chicago Press, 1953.

Gros, Daniel, and Alfred Steinherr. *Winds of Change: Economic Transition in Central and Eastern Europe*. London: Longman, 1995.

International Monetary Fund. *Exchange Arrangements and Exchange Restrictions*. Annual Report. Washington, D.C.: IMF, various years.

———. *Economic Reviews* for Estonia (4), Latvia (6), and Lithuania (7), 1993. Washington, D.C.: IMF, 1993.

James, Harold. *International Monetary Cooperation since Bretton Woods*. New York: Oxford University Press, 1996.

Kaplan, Jacob, and Günther Schleiminger. *The European Payments Union: Financial Diplomacy in the 1950s*. Oxford: Clarendon Press, 1989.

Kindleberger, Charles P. *The Dollar Shortage*. Cambridge, Mass.: The MIT Press, 1950.

Kornai, Janos. *The Road to a Free Economy*. New York: Norton, 1990.

Little, I. M. D., Tibor Scitovsky, and Maurice F. Scott. *Industry and Trade in Some Developing Countries: A Comparative Study*. London: Oxford University Press, 1970.

McKinnon, Ronald I. *The Order of Economic Liberalization: Financial Control in the Transition to a Market Economy*. Baltimore: Johns Hopkins University Press, 1991.

Mussa, Michael. "The Adjustment Process and the Timing of Trade Liberalization." In *Economic Liberalization in Developing Countries*. Ed. Armeane M. Choksi and Demetris Papageorgiou. Oxford: Basil Blackwell, 1986.

———. "Government Policy and the Adjustment Process." In *Import Competition and Response*. Ed. Jagdish N. Bhagwati. Chicago: University of Chicago Press, 1982.

Nurkse, Ragnar. *International Currency Experience*. Geneva: League of Nations, 1944.

OECD. *Exchange Control Policy*. Paris: OECD, 1993.

———. *Integrating Emerging Market Economies into the International Trading System*. Paris: OECD, 1994.

———. *Short-Term Economic Indicators: Transition Economies*. Paris: OECD, quarterly.

Peck, Merton J., Petr Aven, and Thomas Richardson, eds. *What Is to Be Done? Proposals for the Soviet Transition to Market*. New Haven: Yale University Press, 1991.

Russian Federation. *Russian Economic Trends 1995*. Vol. 4, no. 2. London: Whurr Publishers, 1995.

Sachs, Jeffrey. *Poland's Jump to the Market Economy*. Cambridge, Mass.: The MIT Press, 1993.

Triffin, Robert. *Europe and the Money Muddle: From Bilateralism to Near-Convertibility, 1947–1956*. New Haven: Yale University Press, 1957.

———. *The World Money Maze*. New Haven: Yale University Press, 1966.

WEFA Group. *Eurasia Economic Outlook*. Eddystone, Pa.: WEFA Group, 1996.

Wiener Institut für Internationale Wirtschaftsvergleiche (WIIW). *Countries in Transition, 1995*. Vienna, 1996.

Williamson, John, ed. *Currency Convertibility in Eastern Europe*. Washington, D.C.: Institute for International Economics, 1991.

Zloch-Christy, Iliana, ed. *Bulgaria in a Time of Change: Economic and Political Dimensions*. Aldershot: Avebury, 1996.

PART II

CURRENCY BOARD ARRANGEMENTS

3

Why Currency Boards?

Iikka Korhonen, Pekka Sutela, Niina Pautola, and Iliana Zloch-Christy

A SHORT HISTORY OF CURRENCY BOARD ARRANGEMENTS

In the nineteenth century currency boards were common in the British colonies; the first currency board was established in Mauritius in 1849 (Williamson 1995). Eventually there were more than seventy currency boards operating within the British Empire. By using a currency board arrangement instead of the pound sterling, the colonies were able to collect some seignorage. The reserves held by the currency boards could be deposited to earn interest (usually in London), and naturally most of the liabilities (notes and coins) were not interest-bearing.

In addition to the British colonies many independent countries introduced currency boards, especially before the Second World War. For example, Argentina had its first currency board from 1902 to 1914, and Ireland continued to operate a de facto currency board up until the 1970s (Honohan 1994). Ireland had pegged its currency to the pound sterling, which was understandable since Great Britain was by far the most important trading partner of Ireland.

After the Second World War more colonies started to gain independence, and in most instances the authorities of the newly independent countries felt that a currency board was not the most appropriate monetary and exchange rate arrangement. The ability to pursue independent monetary and exchange rate policies was deemed important for achieving economic growth, and since a currency board arrangement meant that the exchange rate or interest rate could not be used as an active instrument in macroeconomic policy, a more flexible exchange rate arrangement was desired.

One could argue that the first "modern" currency board was introduced in Hong Kong. In 1983 Hong Kong reintroduced a currency board after a period of heightened instability in the foreign exchange market. (For an assessment of Hong Kong's currency board, see Kwan and Lui 1996.) The Hong Kong dollar is pegged to the U.S. dollar. In the Hong Kong regime the bank notes are issued by three commercial banks. The commercial banks in turn have to submit U.S. dollars of at least equal value to the Exchange Fund in exchange for certificates of indebtedness. However, over the years Hong Kong has moved away from pure currency board arrangement. In 1988 the Hong Kong Exchange Fund acquired a right to conduct open-market operations and in 1990 a right to issue Treasury bills (Williamson 1995). However, Hong Kong has maintained its strict peg to the U.S. dollar. The peg has also survived the transfer of the political power to the People's Republic of China and the recent turbulence in the world financial markets, although the interest rate spread between Hong Kong and United States has been wide at times.

After Hong Kong the next country to introduce a currency board arrangement was Argentina in 1991, following a severe bout of hyperinflation. Therefore it is perhaps not surprising that the Argentine public was ready to give up the discretionary powers of the monetary authority and to commit to a simple rule-based monetary policy. Introduction of the currency board was successful in reducing inflation.

During 1990s currency boards were introduced in several transition countries, that is, countries that are in the process of transforming their economic system from a largely command-based one to a more market-oriented one and their political systems from totalitarianism to more democratic ones. The first transition country to introduce a currency board arrangement was Estonia in June 1992. Estonia was followed by Lithuania in April 1994 and Bulgaria in June 1997. Also the former Yugoslav republic of Bosnia-Herzegovina has introduced a currency board amid grave political difficulties. All transition countries that have introduced a currency board have done so after severe macroeconomic imbalances. The one possible exception is Lithuania, where the external value of currency had been stabilized before the currency board was implemented, but authorities were concerned that unless a more binding commitment to the fixed exchange rate was introduced, there would be an overwhelming pressure on fiscal policy, and the central bank would have to finance at least part of the resulting deficit (Camard 1996).

During the recent financial crises around the globe currency boards have been proposed as a remedy, but it is interesting that at least so far no large country (after Argentina, that is) has introduced a currency board.

THE FUNCTIONING OF A CURRENCY BOARD

The idea of currency boards was originally developed for the British colonies. Since these historical precedents, several countries, including Argentina, Ireland, Singapore, Malaysia, Hong Kong, and, more recently, Estonia, Lithuania, and Bulgaria, have introduced currency boards. A pure currency board arrangement is not only the strictest form of a fixed exchange rate regime; in fact, it is much more than that. Under a strict currency board, there is no monetary policy. Monetary policy is in essence transferred to a foreign authority and to market forces. The monetary authorities commit to issuing domestic currency only in exchange for a foreign currency at a fixed exchange rate. In principle, the peg can be to a basket of currencies or to a single currency. In practice, all presently operating currency boards have opted for the latter on transparency and simplicity grounds.[1] In addition, the reserve currency is often the currency of the country's main trading partner or more generally the currency that is used most for its international transactions. A currency board requires that official foreign exchange reserves are at least equal, at the given rate of exchange, to the domestic currency issued and usually also to the overall amount of the commercial banks' reserves with the currency board. In other words, domestic notes and coins are issued only if and when they are backed by foreign exchange reserves.

As regards the main differences between a currency board and a traditional central bank, a currency board's balance sheet consists principally of its holdings of the reserve currency on the assets side. On the liabilities side, there is an equal value of cash held by the public and deposits by commercial banks. Currency boards often aim to hold excess reserves in order to guard the risk of a decline in the value of their assets.[2] These excess reserves correspond to the net worth of the currency board. Unlike a currency board, a traditional central bank holds not only foreign but also domestic assets. In most cases, an important part of these domestic assets consists of government debt.

A currency board yields seigniorage, as it earns interest from its holdings of reserve currency securities. The net profit of a currency board corresponds to these interest earnings minus the cost of putting and maintaining notes and coins in circulation and other operating expenses of the board.

Currency boards are generally established by law. This is to guarantee that operations are protected from political interference and lobbying by various interest groups. The main characteristics of a currency board—the adoption of clear and stringent monetary rule and the provision of sufficient foreign exchange reserves to support the system—usually restrain the monetary authorities from extending credit to the government or the banking system. These rigidly upheld principles are practiced under a *pure (strict) currency board arrangement*. However, under a *modified currency board arrangement*, the law provides for some flexibility. The currency board may, for example, provide financial support to banks from its excess reserves, or it can borrow money from international capital markets to do so. The monetary authorities may also issue certificates of deposit or other securities to provide or withdraw liquidity.[3]

A traditional central bank exercises monetary policy by using various monetary policy instruments to change the monetary base. A currency board, in contrast, has no (or only very limited) room for maneuvering in the area of monetary policy. This means that money supply is determined solely (or primarily) by market forces. The monetary base increases only (or, at least, essentially only) when the public sells foreign currency to a currency board at the fixed exchange rate, or when foreign money flows into the country. Conversely, the monetary base decreases when the public sells cash back to a currency board and purchases foreign exchange, or when money flows out of the country.

Under a currency board system, the level of interest rates is also market-determined, either fully under a pure currency board and mostly under a modified currency board, as monetary operations are not permitted (under a pure currency board arrangement), or largely restricted (under a modified currency board arrangement). Consequently, changes in the board's foreign exchange reserves will automatically be felt in domestic liquidity and interest rates. A fall in reserves, that is, a deficit in the combined currency and capital account, tightens domestic liquidity, which ceteris paribus leads to higher interest rates, while a rise in foreign exchange reserves increases domestic liquidity and leads, other things being equal, to lower interest rates.[4] In principle, it is possible to adjust an exchange rate fixed under a currency board. However, this rarely occurs.[5] After all, removing the certainty of the exchange rate, even once, encourages speculation about the prospects for a future re-alignment. As a result, the credibility gained through establishing a currency board would be severely hurt, which would subvert the underlying rationale of setting up such a monetary framework in the first place.

ADVANTAGES AND DISADVANTAGES OF A CURRENCY BOARD ARRANGEMENT

Most advantages and disadvantages of a currency board arrangement[6] are similar to the pros and cons of fixed exchange rate regimes.[7] Here, however, we focus on the specific arguments for and against currency boards, and will not reproduce the debate on fixed versus flexible exchange rate regimes. Nevertheless, when arguing either for or against a currency board arrangement, it is important to bear in mind that the experience with different exchange rate regimes—ranging from flexible to fixed and the different variants in between—has shown that there is no single exchange rate system that would be optimal in all circumstances and at all times.

In practice, there have been various reasons for establishing a currency board. Some countries established a currency board in response to an economic crisis: they wished to end a currency crisis resulting from lost credibility and to support a stabilization and reform program. In other cases, a currency board was established because of limited expertise in monetary management.[8] In general, one of the main motives for installing a currency board is to build up credibility. The system implies the strict prohibition of financing government deficits or of the provision of credits to the banking sector. First, this should encourage sound fiscal policy making, leaving spending cuts, revenue increases, or lending from (domestic or foreign) banks as alternatives to the government. However, it cannot be taken for granted that a currency board arrangement automatically leads to a sound fiscal policy, especially if a country has lacked fiscal discipline in the past. A currency board may also limit moral hazard in the banking system. It may be beneficial not to have a lender of last resort, if crises in the banking system result from poor bank management and supervision.

Since the currency board always has enough reserve currency assets to at least cover its liabilities, it should generally be in a position to effect the conversion into foreign exchange, unlike a central bank whose assets have been run down.[9] A currency board also provides an automatic balance-of-payments adjustment mechanism that essentially functions in the same manner as under the gold standard fixed exchange rate system. If the currency board country's combined current and capital account is in deficit, money supply is reduced and ceteris paribus interest rates rise, which promotes a capital inflow. At the same time, increased domestic interest rates reduce domestic absorption, thereby improving the current account position. However, it is important to distinguish between "movements along the demand curve for a currency" and "shifts in demand." That is, a currency board (and, more generally, any rigidly fixed exchange rate regime) will not be successful in leading to the automatic correction of external imbalances if currency preferences change.[10]

One of the main arguments for currency boards is that they tend to deliver low inflation. In fact, as was discussed earlier, there is some empirical evidence that currency boards are indeed associated with better inflation performance than other forms of pegged exchange rate regimes (even allowing for potential endogeneity of the regime choice). This superior inflation record appears to be mainly due to lower inflationary expectations reflecting, on average, a higher degree of confidence in the currency board regime than in that of standard pegged exchange rate regimes.[11] Empirical studies also point out that currency board countries exhibit a relatively better growth performance than other economies.[12]

Finally, a currency board may have a specific appeal in economies in which foreign currencies are used in parallel to the country's own legal tender ("dollarization"). In such cases, there is an advantage in stabilizing the domestic currency by linking it tightly to that currency (dollar) via a currency board.[13]

All in all, a currency board, if successful, can strengthen the credibility of the monetary authorities, may foster sound fiscal policies, and should lead to lower inflation.

Despite the benefits, currency boards have drawbacks as well. At the outset, it may be difficult for a country to gather sufficient hard currency reserves to back the entire monetary base. This is one of the reasons currency board arrangements are sometimes recommended to small open economies rather than to big countries.

The loss of active monetary policy under a currency board arrangement can have disadvantages. An active monetary policy can be helpful in a variety of situations, for example, in the case of significant capital outflows or inflows. More generally, a purely rule-based regime is inflexible, which is particularly problematic in case of shocks. In addition, the currency board may slow down the learning and reform process in (transition) countries, where both the experience in designing and conducting monetary policy as well as the availability of monetary policy instruments is limited.

Furthermore, a currency board tends to be procyclical: when an economy is doing well, capital flows in, interest rates fall, and this reinforces the economic boom. However, developments can change quickly due to the volatility of capital flows. As soon as capital flows out, interest rates rise, and it will become necessary to tighten fiscal policy.[14] As a consequence, economic growth slows down.

Under a strict currency board regime, monetary authorities cannot act as a lender of last resort, that is, banks cannot ask for any rescue loans to avoid a crisis in the banking system. Although this may be beneficial for the banking system in the longer run, it can limit the room for maneuver for dealing with banking sector crises in the shorter term. However, the experience of modified currency boards disposing of a lender-of-last-resort function suggests that in practice a flexible and extensive use of these funds goes at the expense of the credibility that has been earned as a consequence of sticking to the strict rules of the currency board.[15]

The prohibition of budgetary financing by the currency board does not necessarily force sufficient prudence on fiscal policy making. The government may borrow from international financial markets, provided that a country has access to these markets. Eventually, this may lead to overborrowing. Furthermore, in transition economies with state-owned banks, the government may be tempted to put pressure on these banks to extend credit in crisis situations and to fund this externally. Consequently, the authorities may be tempted to delay privatization of state-owned banks (which may have become the government's "lenders of last resort"). Moreover, there is the problem of real misalignment. If a country's inflation rate remains higher than that of the country to which the currency is pegged, the currency can become overvalued. However, this is only the case if real appreciation outpaces the trend appreciation of the equilibrium real exchange rate that is associated with above-average efficiency gains (which typically characterize the economic developments in catching-up economies). Furthermore, no exchange rate-related competitiveness problem occurs as long as real appreciation is in fact the gradual correction of an earlier undervaluation. Since the exchange rate cannot be altered to help the economy adjust to external shocks, such as a fall in exports or shifts in capital flows, domestic prices and wages must adjust. If, for example, wages are sticky, which they often tend to be, due to binding wage contracts or wage indexation schemes, for example, the risk of the domestic currency becoming overvalued is high. Against this background, measures designed to increase wage flexibility are particularly crucial under a currency board and the strict nominal exchange rate rigidity it entails.[16] If prices and wages are sticky, adjustment to shocks is lengthy and costly in terms of both output and employment.

To summarize, it should be stressed that the main negative impacts of the currency board arrangement on the macroeconomy are as follows:

1. The national currency appreciates in real terms with a negative impact on the country's exports and competitiveness.
2. Trade and current accounts deteriorate.
3. There arises an urgent need of balance-of-payments financing, and external borrowing, thus deteriorating further the external balance.
4. There is a decline in real incomes given the downward pressure on the value of the currency.

NOTES

1. See Balino, Enoch et al. (1997).

2. The value of the currency board's assets can shrink, for example, if interest rates in the reserve currency country rise.

3. Monetary operations under a monitored currency board are usually strictly limited in several ways. Their main aim is to smooth short-term interest rates' volatility in the money market. If the scope for monetary operations is expanded beyond fairly narrow boundaries, the question arises of whether such a revised monetary framework could still be labeled a modified currency board arrangement.

4. In this study, we take the current account, the capital account (excluding reserves), and the change in reserves as the three standard components of the balance of payments.

5. In Hong Kong, for example, there have been periodic discussions over the possibility of realigning the Hong Kong dollar. However, the proposal has always been rejected.

6. See Williamson (1995); Balino, Enoch et al. (1997).

7. For reviews of the literature, see Wickham (1985); Aghevli et al.

(1991); Isard (1995), Chapter 11; International Monetary Fund Institute (1992).

8. Santiprabhob (1997).

9. However, as the foreign reserves of a currency board usually cover only the monetary base and not broad money, this conversion cannot be guaranteed if there is a large-scale bank run during which a major share of deposits in domestic currency are withdrawn and simultaneously converted into foreign exchange.

10. Tschinkel (1998).

11. See Ghosh et al. (1998), who quantify the inflation differential between the currency board and other fixed peg countries as being in the order of 4 percentage points per year.

12. See Ghosh et al. (1998), who conclude that "average annual per capita growth was almost twice as high under currency boards than under floating or pegged exchange rates"; this finding holds across the various per capita income categories.

13. See Liviatan (1993).

14. See Williamson (1995).

15. See Santiprabhob (1997).

16. See Calvo et al. (1997).

REFERENCES

Aghevli, Bijan B., Mohsin S. Khan, and Peter J. Montiel. 1991. *Exchange Rate Policy in Developing Countries: Some Analytical Issues*. IMF occasional paper, no. 78. International Monetary Fund, Washington, D.C. (March).

Backé, Peter. 1997. "Special Report on Bulgaria and Romania." In *Focus on Transition*. Oesterreichische Nationalbank, Vienna. (January): 18–26.

Balino, Tomas J. T., Charles Enoch, et al. 1997. *Currency Board Arrangements: Issues and Experiences*. IMF occasional paper, no. 151. International Monetary Fund, Washington, D.C. (August).

Balyozov, Zdravko. 1997. "Equilibrium Exchange Rates and Foreign Exchange Reserves under a Currency Board Arrangement in Bulgaria." In *Bulgarian National Bank Monthly Bulletin*. (June): 23–27.

Bank of Lithuania. 1997. *Monetary Policy Programme of the Bank of Lithuania for 1997–1999*. Vilnius.

———. 1998. Monthly Bulletin. Vilnius (April).

Bennett, Adam G. G. 1994. *Currency Boards: Issues and Experiences.* IMF paper on policy analysis and assessment, no. 94/18. International Monetary Fund, Washington, D.C. (September).

———. 1993. "The Operation of the Estonian Currency Board." In *IMF Staff Papers* 40(2) (June): 451–70.

Calvo, Guillermo, W. Max Corden, Stanley Fischer, Alan Walters, and John Williamson. 1997. *Currency Boards and External Shocks. How Much Pain, How Much Gain?* World Bank, Washington, D.C. (January).

Camard, Wayne. 1996. *Discretion with Rules? Lessons from the Currency Board Arrangement in Lithuania.* IMF paper on policy analysis and assessment, no. 96/1 International Monetary Fund, Washington, D.C. (March).

Chan, Norman. 1998. *The Currency Board System in Hong Kong.* Paper presented at the International Conference on Exchange Rate Stability and Currency Board Economics, Hong Kong Baptist University, November 28, 1998.

Dietz, Raimund. 1997. "Currency Board Arrangement for Bulgaria: What is a Competitive Level for the Bulgarian Exchange Rate?" In *Bulgarian National Bank Monthly Bulletin* (April): 27–31.

Dobrinsky, Rumen. 1997a. *Transition Failures: Anatomy of the Bulgarian Crisis.* The Vienna Institute research reports, no. 236. The Vienna Institute for Comparative Economic Studies (WIIW) (April).

———. 1997b. "The Currency Board in Bulgaria: First Experience." In *The Vienna Institute Monthly Report.* The Vienna Institute for Comparative Economic Studies (WIIW). (July–August): 12–20.

Dubauskas, Gediminas. 1996. *Monetary and Exchange Rate Policy in Lithuania.* Institute for Advanced Studies Vienna. East European Series, no. 31 (April).

Eesti Pank. 1992. *Monetary Policy Chronicle for the Year of the Monetary Reform.* Tallinn.

———. 1997a. *Inflation and Monetary Policy in Estonia.* Tallinn (May).

———. 1997b. "Estonian Reform Experience and European Developments." In *Five Years of the Estonian Kroon.* Papers of the academic conference held in Tallinn (June 18).

———. 1997c. *Measures for Ensuring Sustainability of the Banking Sector Development.* Press release. http://www.ee/epbe.

———. 1997d. *The 1997–1998 Programme for the Economic Policy of the Government of Estonia and Eesti Pank.* Press release (November 11). http://www.ee/epbe.

European Commission, Directorate-General for Economic and Financial Affairs. 1998. *European Economy—Supplement C: Economic Reform Monitor* (March).

Funke, Michael. 1995. *Importing Central Bank Credibility: The Case of Estonia.* Humboldt Universität zu Berlin discussion paper. Economic Series, no. 56 (July).

Ghosh, Atish R., Anne-Marie Gulde, and Holger C. Wolf. 1998. *Currency Boards: The Ultimate Fix*? IMF working paper, no. 98/8. International Monetary Fund, Washington, D.C. (January).

Honohan, Patrick. 1994. *Currency Board or Central Bank? Lessons from the Irish Pound's Link with Sterling, 1928–79.* Centre for Economic Policy Research discussion paper no. 1040, London.

IMF Institute. 1992. *Approaches to Exchange Rate Policy: Choices for Developing and Transition Economies.* International Monetary Fund, Washington, D.C. (December).

International Monetary Fund. 1998. *World Economic Outlook.* Washington, D.C. (May).

Isard, Peter. 1995. *Exchange Rate Economics.* Cambridge: Cambridge University Press.

Knight, Malcolm, et al. 1997. *Central Bank Reforms in the Baltics, Russia, and the Other Countries of the Former Soviet Union.* IMF occasional paper, no. 157. International Monetary Fund, Washington, D.C. (December).

Korhonen, Iikka. 1996. "Dollarization in Lithuania." In *Review of Economies in Transition,* no. 5. Bank of Finland, Unit for Eastern European Economies, Helsinki: 53–59.

Krzak, Maciej. 1997. "Estonia, Latvia and Lithuania: From Plan to Market—Selected Issues." In *Focus on Transition.* Oesterreichische Nationalbank, Vienna. (February): 22–51.

———. 1996. "Persistent Moderate Inflation in Poland and Hungary." In *Focus on Transition.* Oesterreichische Nationalbank, Vienna. (February): 46–66.

Kwan, Y. and F. Lui. 1996. *Hong Kong's Currency Board and Changing Monetary Regimes.* National Bureau of Economic Research, INC. Cambridge. (August): 1–8.

Law on the Bulgarian National Bank. 1997. (June).

Liviatan, Nissan. 1993. *Proceedings of a Conference on Currency Sub-*

stitution and Currency Boards. World Bank discussion papers, no. 207. World Bank, Washington, D.C.

Manchev, Tzvetan. 1997. "Money Supply in Bulgaria under a Currency Board Arrangement." In *Bulgarian National Bank Monthly Bulletin.* (August): 41–47.

Mihailov, Anton. 1998. Bulgaria: "Radical Break with the Past but No Recovery Yet." In *The Vienna Institute Monthly Report.* The Vienna Institute for Comparative Economic Studies (WIIW). (April): 3–5.

Mihov, Ilian. 1998. "Bulgaria and the Currency Board." In *Europa—Economic Policy Insights for the Associated Countries.* CEPR Economic Policy Initiative, no. 5 (January).

OECD. 1998. *Economic Outlook.* 63 (April).

Oesterreichische Nationalbank. 1997. *Monetary Policy in Transition in East and West: Strategies, Instruments and Transmission Mechanisms.* Conference proceedings, Vienna.

Pautola, Niina, and Sutela, Pekka. 1998. "Eastern Enlargement of the EU: Estonia's Perspective." In MOCT-MOST. *Eastern Enlargement of the European Union: Some Critical Issues for Central and Eastern European Countries* 8(8).

Pou, Pedro. 1998. *Currency Convertibility in Argentina.* Paper presented at the International Conference on Exchange Rate Stability and Currency Board Economics, Hong Kong Baptist University, November 28, 1998.

Rudgalvis, Kestutis. 1996. *Establishing a New Currency and Exchange Rate Determination: The Case of Lithuania.* CERT discussion paper, no. 96/4. Centre for Economic Reform and Transformation. Heriot-Watt University, Edinburgh.

Saavalainen, Tapio. 1995. *Stabilization in the Baltic Countries: A Comparative Analysis.* IMF working paper, no. 95/44. International Monetary Fund, Washington, D.C. (April).

Santiprabhob, Veerathai. 1997. *Bank Soundness and Currency Board Arrangements: Issues and Experience.* IMF paper on policy analysis and assessment, no. 97/11. International Monetary Fund, Washington, D.C. (December).

Stupar, Holger. 1998. "Bulgarien—Aufschwung durch Currency Board." In *Osteuropa-Perspektiven* (March): 26–32.

Tschinkel, Sheila. 1998. "Prerequisites for Successful Fixed Exchange Rate Arrangements for Emerging Market Economies." Lecture given at The Vienna Institute for Comparative Economic Studies. Vienna (April 23).

Viilman, Natalja. 1997. *The Evaluation of the Real Exchange Rate of the Estonian Kroon on the Basis of Different Indicators*. Eesti Pank Papers, no. 1. Tallinn.

Vladimirov, Boris. 1998. "Osteuropäische Finanzmärkte: Bulgarien auf Reformkurs." *Bankarchiv* 45(4): 295–99.

Wickham, Peter. 1985. "The Choice of Exchange Rate Regime in Developing Countries." In *IMF Staff Papers* 33(2) (June): 248–88.

Williamson, John. 1995. *What Role for Currency Boards*? Policy Analyses in International Economics, no. 40. Institute for International Economics, Washington, D.C. (September).

Wyplosz, Charles. 1997. "Monetary Policy Options for the 'Outs.' " Oesterreichische Nationalbank.

Zarazaga, Carlos E. 1995. "Argentina, Mexico, and Currency Boards: Another Case of Rules Versus Discretion. Federal Reserve Bank of Dallas." *Economic Review* 4: 14–24.

4

Currency Boards in International Perspective

Niina Pautola

Comparative analysis of currency boards (see Table 4.1) shows that although there are differences between countries in terms of, for example, economic history and the reasons for the establishment of the currency board, market participation by the currency authority, or lender of last resort arrangements, the fundamentals of the system remain the same. Furthermore, there are certain economic principles that apply to every currency board country. This chapter draws some conclusions in regard to currency boards in international perspective—what have we learned from currency boards and what the likely future prospects of currency boards are. (The main features of currency board arrangements in Estonia, Lithuania, Bulgaria, Argentina, and Hong Kong are summarized in Table 4.1.)

First, one of the key arguments for currency boards is to avoid inflation. A country ties its currency to a low-inflation currency, makes a firm commitment, and, as a result, achieves low inflation. However, it is important to remember that the fixed exchange rate gives roughly the same rate of inflation only in tradable goods, which provides the price anchor. The overall inflation rate is, however, an average of tradables and nontradables. When inflation in tradables is fixed, the inflation rate of nontradables will be determined by the relative productivity growth in nontradable sectors of goods and services vis-à-vis tradables. This explains why a currency board country may have relatively high inflation

Table 4.1
Comparative Analysis: Currency Boards in Estonia, Lithuania, Bulgaria, Argentina, and Hong Kong

	Estonia	Lithuania	Bulgaria
Establishment of a currency board	June 1992 As a result of the stabilization program	April 1994 As a result of a lively debate over the monetary framework	July 1997 As a result of financial crisis and unsuccessful stabilization
Currency peg	IDM = 8EEK	1USD = 4LTL	1DM = 1,000LEV
Administrative structure	1) The Issues Department: responsible for operating the currency board 2) The Banking Department: responsible for managing excess foreign reserves	Bank of Lithuania responsible for administering the currency board	1) The Issue Department: responsible for running the currency board 2) The Banking Department: lender of last resort 3) Banking Supervision Department
Backing rule	100% of monetary base	100% of currency and the central bank's liquid liabilities	100% of monetary base
Assets eligible for backing	Foreign assets, initially by gold and shortly thereafter by DM interest-bearing assets	Foreign assets and gold	Foreign assets and gold
LOLR (Lender of Last Resort)	Assistance to troubled financial institutions limited to surplus foreign exchange reserves	Liquidity loans to commercial banks from excess reserves, primarily to large banks whose bankruptcy would carry a systemic risk for the financial sector	So far there has been no need for LOLR
Credit to government	Prohibited	Prohibited	Prohibited

Table 4.1 (*continued*)

	Estonia	Lithuania	Bulgaria
Market participation and instruments	Participation in the foreign exchange market, central bank bills, reserve requirements, a standing deposit facility	Reserve requirements to regulate liquidity, short-term credit facilities for commercial banks, new instruments since the beginning of 1997	Minimum reserve requirements; not actively used, remained the same since January 1997
Banking crisis	1992	1995 and early 1996	1996 and early 1997
Developments since the establishment of the currency board	Increase in foreign reserves, pressures in 1994, 1995, and 1997. Especially in 1997: large trade and current account deficit, economic boom, substantial domestic credit expansion. Still relatively high inflation, real exchange rate appreciation. Slowdown of economic activity in 1998 due to the measures taken by the Bank of Estonia to limit commercial bank credit and to protect/strengthen banks' balance sheets.	Rapid growth in reserve money right after the establishment of the currency board, pressures 1994 and 1995, problem with shaken credibility and devaluation rumors, high inflation, increasing trade and current account deficit, high interest rates, the real appreciation of the LTL (Lithuanian litas).	The significant increase in official foreign exchange reserves reflecting 1997's favorable balance-of-payments developments, increase in bank deposits, improved fiscal performance, improved tax collection.
Results of the currency board and future perspectives	Falling inflation, economic growth, increase in public's and foreign investors' confidence, sound fiscal policy, capital inflows, reduction in	Falling inflation, lower interest rates, economic recovery, reduced degree of dollarization, sound fiscal performance less pronounced. At the end of 1996	Falling inflation, increase in economic activity, fallen interest rates, increased FDI, current and trade accounts in surplus. 1997 BNB

Table 4.1 (*continued*)

	Estonia	Lithuania	Bulgaria
	interest rates. Since January 1999, the exchange rate of Estonian kroon against German mark has remained on the previous level 8:1. Since the beginning of 1999, the Estonian kroon has been fixed against the euro in accordance with the conversion rate of the German mark against the euro determined on December 31, 1998.	authorities decided that mainly for integration reasons, Lithuania should exit the currency board: a three-stage plan to abandon the currency board took effect at the beginning of 1997.	(Bulgarian National Bank) Law: the lev's link to the DM will be replaced by a euro peg "when the euro becomes legal tender in Germany."

	Argentina	Hong Kong
Establishment of a currency board	March 1991 History of monetary instability, hyperinflation in 1989	October 1983 The start of the negotiations over the future of Hong Kong in 1982 led to a series of financial crises: stock market crash, real estate price collapse, runs of small banks, and rapid depreciation of the HK dollar.
Currency peg	1 USD = 1 Argentine peso[a]	1 USD = 7.8 HKD
Administrative structure	Central Bank of Argentine Republic	Exchange Fund (EF) under the supervision of the Hong Kong Monetary Authority. Before December 1996, interbank settlement system was taken care of by the settlement institution, a commercial bank (Hong Kong and Shanghai

Table 4.1 (*continued*)

	Argentina	Hong Kong
		Banking Corporation), not by a central bank or monetary authority.
LOLR	Argentina's central bank can issue money up to the level that would push the MB/FR ratio above 1.25. In April 1995, legislation was passed that allowed the central bank to provide liquidity assistance in the case of systemic liquidity problems without impairing the backing of monetary liabilities.	Liquidity Adjustment Facility introduced in 1992. Under this facility, banks having liquidity problems may borrow overnight money from the Exchange Fund through repo transactions of eligible securities: Exchange Fund paper and other high-quality private-sector debt securities.
Backing rule	First, 100% of monetary base, later, in 1995, the convertibility law was changed and the flexibility in the backing clauses was increased, allowing the central bank to back up 33% of its monetary liabilities with Argentine government securities.	100%, three commercial note-issuing banks issue Hong Kong dollar bank notes against holdings of certificates of indebtedness (CIs) issued by the Exchange Fund. The note-issuing banks are required by law to hold CIs as a cover for the bank notes they issue.
Assets eligible for backing	Foreign assets, gold, and the U.S. dollar denominated Argentine government debt	Foreign assets
Market participation and Instruments	Traditional reserve requirement policy fully backed by international reserves. Before the Tequila crisis, there was high reserve requirement for demand deposits, but low for time deposits. During the crisis, the major deposit withdrawals were in time deposits. This led to an introduction of changes to the banking liquidity policy:	Series of monetary reforms in 1988. The main aim was to improve the discipline in the management of interbank liquidity. The HKMA can assist in maintaining the external value of the currency through the "accounting arrangements."[b] These permit the Exchange Fund to bring pressure to bear

Table 4.1 (*continued*)

	Argentina	Hong Kong
	homogenization and strengthening of the requirements. During the Tequila crisis of 1995, a way was also found to create deposit insurance without public funds, by making the banks bear the full cost of the insurance. Furthermore, to enhance international liquidity, the central bank signed a contingent repurchase agreement facility with a number of major international banks.	on interbank liquidity. The HKMA has also issued bills so that it can influence rates through open market operations. In addition, the HKMA has introduced a discount window (June 1992)=Liquidity Adjustment Facility, which gives more control over short-term interbank interest rates.[c] Finally, the HKMA has been given a right to levy deposit charges.[d] Introduction of the Real Time Gross Settlement interbank payment system.[e]
Banking crisis and shocks	January 1995, Bank Extrader, heavily exposed in Mexican bonds and securities, was closed by the central bank. The fear that other banks were similarly exposed translated into a generalized banking panic and capital flight. Attack against the banking system became attack against the currency. Devaluation rumors strengthened as Mexico had done so shortly before. By the end of April 1995, the financial system had lost 18% of the deposits it had before the Mexican peso devaluation.	Shocks, such as the Gulf War in 1990, the collapse of the European exchange rate mechanism in 1992 and 1993, or the Tequila crisis in 1994, had less effect than was originally expected. The role of political shocks important (the People's Republic of China). Various speculative attacks from October 1997 until the end of 1998. Despite the shocks, the currency board system has been kept in place, but redesigned according to the changing market circumstances.[f]
Developments since the establishment of the currency board	Contrary to the presumption, the currency board did not protect against a speculative attack on the Argentine peso. A devaluation was prevented,	During the 1984–94 period, average GDP growth was 6.4%, the trade surplus was 7.7 of GDP, the budget surplus averaged 2.1% GDP,

Table 4.1 (*continued*)

	Argentina	Hong Kong
	but the price was a severe financial panic and banking crisis. Consequently, measures were taken to strengthen the banking system: stricter capital requirements, introduction of a capital requirement for market risk (value at risk), creation of a deposit insurance institution.	inflation was 7.7% between 1982 and 1994. In 1991–94, real interest rates became negative and, consequently, Hong Kong suffered a boom in asset prices. Due to the Asian crisis, instability in the Russian and Latin American markets, and a contraction in domestic activities,[g] technical measures were adopted to strengthen the currency board arrangement.
Results of the currency board and future perspectives	Prices have become increasingly more flexible downward, as the credibility of the currency has risen. CB has also resulted in lower inflation and economic growth. The lesson from the Tequila crisis of 1995 was that a currency board could survive a massive capital outflow. After the crisis, Argentina was able to recover relatively quickly.	The solidity of Hong Kong dollar has been mainly due to larger reserves which have been far beyond the 100% backup rule. Much of the surplus reserves is a consequence of persistent budgetary surpluses (around 2% of GDP 1987–94). Free trade and liberal regime.

[a]Initially, the exchange rate was set at 10,000 australs per one U.S. dollar. In January 1993, however, the peso was introduced as the new currency (Santiprabhob 1997).

[b]According to this arrangement, the HSBC (Hong Kong's interbank settlement institution until 1996) had to open an account with the Exchange Fund. The purpose was to ensure that the net clearing balance maintained by other banks with the HSBC would not be greater than the balance in the HSBC's account maintained with the Exchange Fund, which was determined by the government. In other words, the maximum amount of liquidity in the interbank market was set. In case the HSBC lent more than this limit, a penal interest rate would be charged. This way, the interbank liquidity was put under the discipline of the currency board system through the Exchange Fund.

[c]Under this facility, banks having liquidity problems may borrow overnight money from the Exchange Fund through repo transactions of eligible securities: Exchange Fund paper and other high-quality private-sector debt securities.

[d]It seems that the HKMA has most of the instruments of a normal central bank. Where to draw the line—what type of system can still be considered a currency board?

[e]Under this rule, every licensed bank in Hong Kong is required to open a clearing account directly with the HKMA. This also implied that the accounting arrangements introduced earlier to indirectly control the interbank liquidity were abolished.

[f]For example, at the end of 1997, banks were given a greater assurance of their access to the liquidity adjustment facility. In addition, since June 1998, the forecast change in the level of interbank liquidity (resulting from the foreign exchange transactions conducted by the HKMA) has been published. This provides commercial banks a signal on the changes in the liquidity conditions.

[g]The HKMA provides a clear undertaking to all licensed banks in Hong Kong to convert the HK dollar in their clearing accounts into U.S. dollars at the fixed exchange rate of HK$7.75 to US$. This reflects the government's commitment to the linked exchange rate regime. The rate of the "Convertibility Undertaking" will be gradually moved to 7.80 starting in April 1999. Another technical measure is the replacement of the then Liquidity Adjustment Facility (LAF) by a Discount Window (DW) with the Base Rate (former LAF Offer Rate) to be determined from time to time by the HKMA. Banks have unrestricted access to the DW for repo transactions using the Exchange Fund bills and notes, which are fully backed by foreign reserves. Those banks who use other papers will continue to be subject to the "repeated borrowing" restriction. Repeated borrowers are those who have borrowed through DW on eight occasions in any period of twenty-five days or on four days in which the DW is open. Repeated borrowers may be charged a penal interest rate.

although its currency is pegged to a low-inflation country's currency. For example, high productivity growth in the nontradables sector was one of the reasons for high inflation in Hong Kong during the 1983–95 period.

Second, the lack of credibility or doubt about it explains, to a large extent, why currency boards are subject to speculative attacks. From this point of view, one must ask how financial market participants view the monetary policy actions: Do they perceive them as temporary and justifiable (the expansion of the monetary base through the central bank's discount window despite declining foreign reserves), or as something similar that has led to devaluation (or a series of devaluations) in the past? It seems that formal institutions or laws cannot remove skepticism about governments' ability to carry out commitments if they have repeatedly been broken in the past. Even with a strong macroeconomic performance, consolidating credibility may take time.

Third, when currency boards are subject to speculative attacks, devaluation can be avoided, but usually only at the cost of financial crisis. This was the case, for example, in Argentina. The combination of a fixed exchange rate, a current account deficit, large short-term international debt, and a weak banking system explains why Argentina became the victim of the Tequila effect, even though it had a currency board regime. Consequently, Argentina suffered from capital outflow. At the end, the country avoided a full collapse of confidence, but suffered from a deep financial crisis, recession, and high unemployment.

An additional observation related to devaluation is that in principle, if there is no explicit or implicit currency denomination mismatch, then the devaluation improves banks' balance sheets. The devaluation can improve balance sheets if you have an external shock and a certain loss becomes nonperforming, so devaluation can (in a way) liquidate the debt. Devaluation also helps stimulate the demand for deposits, and it can prevent runs of banks. However, if bank liabilities are dollarized, as was the case in Argentina where a large share of deposits were in dollars, then a devaluation that affects the real exchange rate will have a negative effect on the health of the financial system.

Fourth, as has been learned, labor market flexibility and coordination is crucial under the currency board regime. Given the argument of labor market flexibility, the exchange rate should be fixed in a country/within an area in which there is factor mobility (labor and capital). However, this is easier said than done: How to bring about labor market flexibility? Would it actually be possible to convince politicians or trade unions that in the long run workers are going to be just as well off with nominal wage flexibility downward as by sticking to nominal wage levels while nominal demand declines when there is, for example, a capital outflow?

Another crucial question related to currency board economies is how to deal or avoid credit squeeze/capital flights? After all the number of tools available is limited. Argentina, for example, responded by lowering the banks' reserve requirements during the run of deposits. The example of Hong Kong shows in turn that modifications in the regulatory structure can reduce the need for a lender of last resort. In addition, permitting the internationalization of the financial sector can help both to reduce the vulnerability of banks to negative external shocks and to smooth out capital flows (because foreign-owned subsidiaries can draw from credit lines to their parent banks when confronted with negative external shocks). A country can avoid capital inflow–outflow shocks, to some extent at least, by also making a government run on a budget deficit or by borrowing abroad. Indeed, some fiscal flexibility has proved to be useful under the currency board regime. In case of adverse-terms-of-trade shock or a capital outflow problem, it helps if a government can engage in temporary fiscal expansion, which could involve more foreign debt. This would offset, partly, the domestic deflationary effects resulting otherwise from the currency board arrangement. However, not all countries have permanent access to the international capital market. Given this, a government might find it useful to have a systemic liquidity policy, which would take into account the short-term liabilities of both the private and the public sector, in both local and foreign currency. All in all, there seems to be a some kind of trade-off between the use of reserves to support convertibility and maintain credibility or to support the banking system. Can a country have a currency board with a credible commitment to a fixed exchange rate, and simultaneously enough room for maneuvering in terms of banking and monetary policy? Perhaps with high enough excess reserves and access to credit, a country could actually have it both ways.

Finally, in addition to the general discussion of currency board arrangements, EU integration and future enlargement have raised a whole new set of questions related to the future perspectives of the currency boards in Central and Eastern Europe. In particular, it has been discussed whether a currency board is an appropriate monetary framework for joining the EU, and, eventually, for participation in the euro zone. In general, there is no obvious reason why a central bank that runs a currency board should not be in a position to fulfill all the requirements the Treaty on European Union lays down in the area of central bank independence. In regards to price stability as the primary objective of central bank policy, a currency board has no policy tools at its disposal to directly fight inflation. However, empirical evidence has shown that a currency board tends to deliver low inflation or even price stability. Monetary policy cooperation among EU countries is based on the existence of market-based monetary policy instruments, and on their effective use, if the need arises. Under a pure currency board regime, there is no (active) monetary policy. Furthermore, a currency board country cannot fully participate in an institutionalized exchange rate cooperation of a standard EU type, which requires flexible use of interest rates. Since a currency board does not allow for any direct control of price level and interest rate developments, meeting the monetary convergence criteria can also become more complicated. So far, Lithuania is the only Eastern European currency board country that has officially announced the exit program. Technically, exit would mean moving away from the strict concept of a currency board and loosening of the backing rule, thereby building up more room to act as a lender of last resort in any future crisis. However, the main problem related to exit is that of credibility. A lot will depend on how well the monetary authorities deal with their new monetary freedom.

To conclude, given the experience with and effects of international economic crisis, turbulence in worldwide capital markets, transition in Central and Eastern Europe, and EU integration, the appropriateness and long-term viability of currency boards will require continuous monitoring and reassessing in the years to come.

REFERENCE

Santiprabhob, Veerathai. 1997. *Bank Soundness and Currency Board Arrangement: Issues and Experience*. IMF paper on policy analysis and assessment, no. 97/11. International Monetary Fund, Washington, D.C. (December).

5

Currency Boards in the Baltics

Iikka Korhonen and Pekka Sutela

This chapter examines currency boards in two Baltic countries, Estonia and Lithuania. Estonia was the first transition economy to introduce a currency board system in 1992. The reasons why Estonia actually chose to introduce a currency board, which was at the time usually regarded as a historical peculiarity of little actual relevance, are still subject to some historical dispute. But beyond reasonable doubt is the fact that the currency board has served Estonia well. Few would have expected in June 1992 that the Estonian currency board would still exist with the original exchange rate of eight Estonian kroons to one German mark almost seven years later. Furthermore, currency boards are no longer regarded as historical peculiarities. Argentina had adopted one even before Estonia. Among the transition economies, Lithuania, Bosnia-Herzegovina, and Bulgaria have all followed the example, and the pros and cons of a currency board have also been debated in the case of Russia, Indonesia and others. One point of view argues that in the long run, only the polar exchange rate regimes—either free float or a currency board—are feasible, in particular for open economies with a history of lost monetary policy credibility.

Such arguments are probably not shared by most economists. They perhaps reflect a puritan approach that is ill at home in a complex world. Whatever our view on that, the least that must be said on the basis of experience recently gained is that a currency board is a genuine alternative that has to be seriously considered. The two Baltic countries with a currency board, Estonia and Lithuania, are small and little-known economies. The interesting questions arise: What is actually their experience? Did they manage their macroeconomies better than, say, Latvia, their common neighbor? Comparing Estonia, Latvia, and Lithuania comes as close to a laboratory experiment as is usually possible in social sciences. And if—as is the case in Estonia and Lithuania—a currency board and a relatively good macro performance go hand in hand, is there a causality? Why does Estonia want to retain the currency board, while Lithuania has announced that it will exit from the arrangement? Can conclusions be drawn for other countries?

These are only some of the questions that should be asked. Not all of them can be addressed here, given the limitations of this chapter. But at least we hope to be able to shed some light on these developments.

The chapter is organized as follows. In the first part we look at the monetary reforms in Estonia and Lithuania. Then we assess how the currency boards have affected the overall economic development in these countries. The final part offers concluding remarks.

MONETARY REFORMS IN ESTONIA AND LITHUANIA

The three Baltic countries gained their independence from the Soviet Union in the latter half of 1991. Lithuania was the first Baltic country to declare independence, but Latvia and Estonia soon followed. Economic reforms had been begun in the Soviet Union already at the end of the 1980s, and these reforms were also implemented in the three Baltic republics. For example, the first commercial bank in the Soviet Union was established in Estonia in 1989 (Korhonen 1996).

One important component in the economic reforms of the Baltic countries was currency reform. (The present discussion on currency reforms draws heavily on Lainela and Sutela [1994].) At the start of 1992 most prices were freed in Russia, and the monthly inflation quickly jumped to over 30 percent as prices rose to eliminate the monetary overhang.[1] After the first initial change in the price level, the monthly inflation was approximately 10 percent during the first half of 1992. In June the monthly inflation rate jumped to almost 30 percent and stayed there for almost five months. Naturally the external value of the ruble depreciated strongly during this period. During the first half of 1992 the Baltic countries were still part of the ruble area, and the apparent instability of the ruble prompted them to look for alternative monetary arrangements. In addition to this the three newly independent countries naturally wanted to assert their independence also in the monetary sphere.

In the end all the Baltic countries chose a fixed exchange rate regime. As is explained in more detail below, Estonia was the first to do this, followed by Latvia and Lithuania. In Latvia and Lithuania the pegging of the currencies was preceded by at least somewhat managed floating.

Why would a country choose to give up the exchange rate as a policy instrument and opt for a fixed exchange rate regime? The analytical literature on the desirability of fixed exchange rates can be said to begin with Mundell (1961). It is generally agreed (see, for example, Isard 1995 and the references therein) that when countries are more open to foreign trade, they have more to gain from fixed exchange rates. In an open economy changes in exchange rate translate faster into changes in nominal wages and prices, and thus exchange rate policy is not so effective in maintaining external balance. At the same time movements in exchange rate threaten domestic price stability. One could argue that smaller countries are natural candidates for a fixed exchange rate as they are more likely to be open to international trade. The currency of a small country may also not be very effective in the traditional functions of money, that is, as a unit of account and medium of exchange. Fixing the currency of a small country to a more widely known currency could enhance its usefulness in the aforementioned functions.

Obviously all Baltic economies are small. The 1998 annual nominal GDP was approximately $5.5 billion in Estonia, $6 billion in Latvia, and $10.5 billion in Lithuania. They are also extremely open. The combined value of exports and imports in 1997 was 157 percent of GDP in Estonia, 81 percent in Latvia, and 104 percent in Lithuania. In addition to this the imports and especially exports of services are quite important for all Baltic countries. Therefore one could argue that the Baltic countries are natural candidates for a regime of fixed exchange rates.

Fixed exchange rates can become overvalued. For example, if wage growth exceeds the growth in productivity for an extended period, domestic producers will lose their competitiveness in export markets. If nominal wages are inflexible downward, then the fastest way to change real wages and restore international competitiveness is to devalue the currency.

Wages could rise exceptionally fast because of large capital inflows, which may cause a boom in domestic lending, inflate the value of assets in the economy, and create a large increase in domestic demand. Capital flows could increase because of financial deregulation, for example, as has happened in several countries around the globe. When capital flows stop or perhaps even reverse, and if the domestic prices and wages do not adjust downward, a country might need to adjust its exchange rate or face an economic downturn. Volatility in asset prices can also cause problems in the banking sector, if banks are exposed to asset prices, either directly or through their loan customers. In principle these problems could be countered with right economic policies, such as better supervision of banks and tighter fiscal policy, but in practice policy makers have often found it difficult to respond in advance to imbalances.

The Baltic countries and especially Estonia can also be used as an example of this sort of asset bubble. In 1997 the equity and real estate prices rose rapidly until September, after which the Tallinn Stock Exchange's Talse index decreased 81 percent by the end of 1998. However, in Estonia the currency board and fixed exchange rate appear to have withstood the different stages of economic cycle so far. In Lithuania the inflow of foreign capital was never as pronounced as in Estonia and correspondingly the increases and decreases in asset prices not as large.

Estonia

Here we present a general view on the currency Board in Estonia. A detailed analysis follows in chapter 6. Estonia was the first Baltic country to introduce its own currency, the kroon. After deliberations the Estonian authorities decided to adopt a currency board system. This was regarded as a quick way to gain confidence for a currency. This consideration weighted quite heavily in the case of Estonia, which was starting a completely new currency in a complex and fragile economic and political situation.

In May 1992 the Estonian parliament passed three laws regarding monetary and exchange rate policy. These were the currency law, the law on backing of the Estonian kroon, and the foreign exchange law (Eesti Pank 1992). These laws define the Estonian currency board and its operating procedures. Estonia didn't adopt the strictest possible version of a currency board, as the Bank of Estonia has some discretion as to how much of the capital inflows are allowed to boost the monetary base. In addition the Bank of Estonia has also kept minimum reserve requirements for commercial banks, something which is not in accordance with the strictest interpretations of a currency board system.[2] However, the foreign currency reserves must at all times cover the currency in circulation and the deposits of commercial banks at the central bank

Figure 5.1
Monthly Inflation Rates in the Baltic Countries

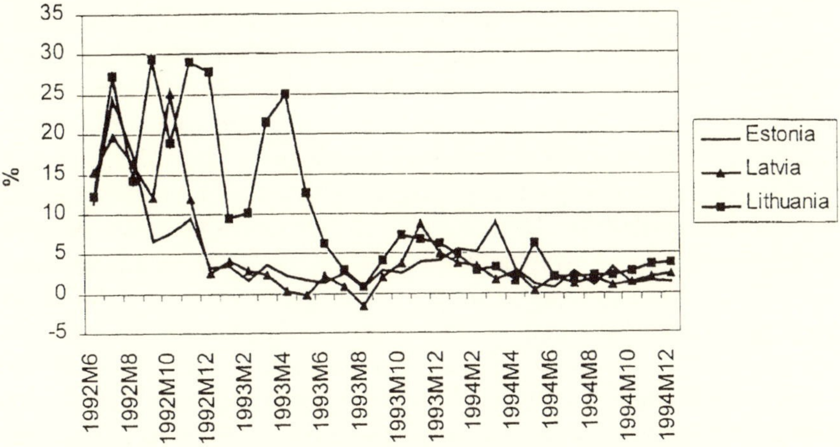

(in practice the Bank of Estonia has kept the reserve coverage generally around 110 percent). The Estonian kroon was pegged to the German mark at the rate IDM = 8EEK. The currency reform was carried out in June 1992. Estonia received its prewar gold reserves (as either gold or foreign exchange) from the Bank of England and other central banks. These reserves then formed the initial backing for the kroon (Bennett 1992).

From the beginning of the monetary reform the kroon was in practice totally convertible for current account purposes. The Bank of Estonia demanded that exporters surrender their export earnings within two months, but it is not clear how strictly this was implemented. Currency deposits were allowed, but no new currency deposits were to be opened. This regulation was finally repealed in March 1994. After this Estonia had full convertibility of its currency and virtually free movement of capital.[3] The exchange rate arrangement was quite successful in bringing the inflation rate initially down, especially when compared to other countries of the former Soviet Union, including the other two Baltic countries. Figure 5.1 shows the monthly inflation rates for the three Baltic countries from June 1992 to December 1994. One can see how Latvia and especially Estonia succeeded in bringing inflation down fairly quickly, but Lithuania struggled considerably longer with high and variable inflation. The example of Latvia shows that disinflation is naturally possible also with more conventional exchange rate arrangements, although the shift in the price level during the latter half of 1992 was clearly larger in

Latvia. Latvian currency (first the Latvian ruble and then the lats) floated from its introduction to the spring of 1994, although the central bank apparently intervened in the market often. In the spring of 1994 the lats was pegged to the Special Drawing Right (SDR) of the IMF.

Further evidence of the credibility of Estonia's new exchange rate regime can be gleaned from the capital movements after the introduction of the new currency. During the latter half of 1992 the Bank of Estonia's foreign assets increased by $135 million, but this was partly caused by restoration of pre war gold and thus cannot be treated as a proper sign of increased confidence. During 1993 the foreign assets of the Bank of Estonia increased by $133 million, which is almost 6 percent of 1993 GDP. This inflow of capital can be partly explained by the privatization method chosen in Estonia. In Estonia many companies were sold on a cash-basis to foreign investors, and this took place mainly between November 1992 and November 1994 (Korhonen et al. 1999). Naturally foreign investors are keenly interested in macroeconomic stability, and in Estonia the currency board regime greatly contributed to this in the early years of transition.

Lithuania

Lithuania and Latvia opted for a more gradual approach to monetary reform. The Lithuanian parliament accepted a law on national currency in December 1991, but political debates about the new currency prevented Lithuania from leaving the ruble zone for some time. In May 1992 the Lithuanian authorities introduced an interim currency, which didn't even have a name, although it was called a coupon (talonas in Lithuanian). This was originally issued at par with the Russian ruble. In September authorities began to withdraw rubles from circulation, and from the beginning of October the use of the ruble was forbidden. In June 1993 the authorities announced the introduction of the new currency, the litas. After July the talonas ceased to be legal tender, and also the use of foreign currencies was banned. The litas was convertible for current account purposes, but Lithuania has retained more restrictions on capital account transactions than the other two Baltic states.

At the beginning of economic reforms Lithuania differed from the other Baltic countries also in its exchange rate arrangement, as Lithuania had a dual exchange rate system until the autumn of 1993. Thanks to lax monetary policy (for example, between the first quarter of 1993 and the first quarter of 1994 the monetary aggregate M1 rose by 134 percent), inflation in Lithuania was considerably higher than in Estonia or Latvia. High inflation was naturally reflected in the external value of Lithuanian currency: talonas depreciated markedly against the dollar up until the summer of 1993, after which the tighter monetary policy succeeded in stopping the depreciation and litas actually appreciated during the summer. Inflation came down drastically during the summer, although there was a clear rebound in monthly inflation toward the end of 1993.

Partly because of the observed volatility of the exchange rate and the low credibility of the monetary policy, debate about the appropriate exchange rate regime intensified in the autumn of 1993. As a result of these discussions, Lithuania decided to adopt a currency board in March 1994, and the new arrangement became effective in April. The litas was pegged to the U.S. dollar at the rate 1USD = 4LTL. Even after the introduction of the currency board Lithuania continued to experience higher inflation than Estonia or Latvia, although currently Lithuania's inflation is as low as Latvia's.

In Lithuania the inflow of capital after the introduction of the currency board was as high as in Estonia, relative to the size of the economy. In 1994 the foreign assets of the Bank of Lithuania increased by $180 million, or almost 7 percent of 1994 GDP. If capital inflows are positively correlated with investors' confidence in the economic policies of a given country, then the new foreign exchange rate regime in Lithuania seems to have been associated with an increase in the credibility of the economic policies.

THE MACROECONOMIC EFFECTS OF THE BALTIC CURRENCY BOARDS

In this section we inspect the macroeconomic effects of the currency board arrangements on the Baltic countries. The most interesting question is whether the countries with currency boards can be claimed to have better macroeconomic performance than countries with other types of exchange rate arrangements. It seems that in stopping the decline in output the currency board may have had some positive effect insofar as it has helped to reduce inflation to low double digits. In reducing inflation the track record of currency boards in the Baltic countries is mixed. For example, Latvia has been able to reduce its annual inflation to under 3 percent (at least for the time being) without a currency board.[4] One important macroeconomic effect of the currency boards has been their disciplinary effect on public finances. As currency boards prohibit the monetary financing of public-sector deficit, they can probably be credited with the relatively low observed deficits in Lithuania and especially in Estonia. (Also here one should remember that Latvia has been able to maintain low deficits without a currency board. In Estonia the central government is forbidden to run a deficit.) However, when assessing the effects of currency boards, one is confronted with the problem of direction of causality. Did Estonia have low public deficits because it was constrained by the currency board arrangement, or did it have both currency board and low deficits because this was desired by all Estonian authorities?

Output

All transition economies started their transformation toward a more market-based economy with a large drop in output. Some have claimed that overtly tight monetary and fiscal policies were behind this drop in output, but when one considers the wide variety of policy stances in Central and Eastern European countries (CEEC) and in the former Soviet Union it becomes evident that the output drop cannot be explained by the conventional demand-management arguments. Gomulka (1998) argues that large supply and demand side shocks caused output to fall. The old economic system produced goods that consumers were not willing to buy, and thus reallocation of resources was needed. Because this cannot be accomplished quickly, output will contract before expanding again. In addition to this the old trade ties between different companies were severed as central planning broke down, and it took time for companies to find both new customers and suppliers.

In all the countries of the former Soviet Union the output contraction has been large—in many cases over 50 percent of the output level at the beginning of transition. Even if one takes into account the fact that at the start of transition the statistics probably overstated the level of production and after the start of the transition they failed to take into account much of the new private sector, the drop in output is sizable. In Latvia and Lithuania the output collapse in 1992 was even larger than in Russia or Ukraine, although subsequent economic performance has been considerably better. In Estonia the initial output drop was not larger than in other countries of the former Soviet Union, even though the monetary and fiscal policies were obviously tighter than in most other countries, and Baltic countries were the first among the former Soviet Union countries to experience GDP growth. In this sense the currency board ar-

Figure 5.2
Level of GDP in the Baltic Countries, Russia, and Ukraine

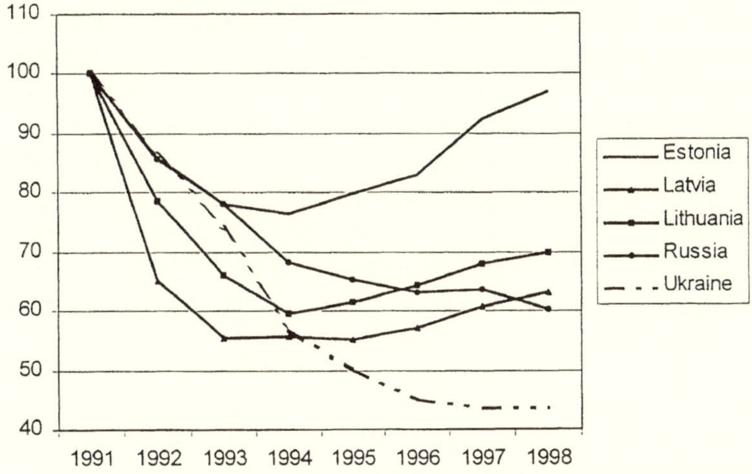

rangements are at least correlated with relatively good economic performance. Figure 5.2 shows the level of GDP in the Baltic countries, Russia, and Ukraine from 1991 to 1998.

However, the currency board (and monetary policy in general) is obviously just one part of the economic policy package. Can the currency board be credited with this early resumption in growth? Early studies concerning output decline and growth in transition economies have usually argued that growth seems to have restarted only after the annual inflation rate has been pushed to low double digits. Excessive inflation rates are detrimental to growth, as they make the economic environment generally more uncertain. Insofar as currency boards have helped to reduce inflation, they have had a positive effect on the level of economic activity. We will return to the role of the currency boards in reducing inflation below.

Since the initial decline in output has been halted, Estonia and Lithuania have posted high GDP growth figures, as has Latvia. These growth rates can be compared to the Polish experience after its initial output decline ended, although at the moment it seems that economic growth is decelerating in the Baltic countries. Estonia and Lithuania have implemented a host of economic policies conducive to growth. First, in both countries the structural reforms progressed quite rapidly, especially in comparison to the other former Soviet Union countries. Most reforms were taken quite early in the transition process. If one would take the average of the transition indicators[5] in EBRD (1994) as a proxy for progress in transition by mid-1994, Estonia (with Hungary, Poland, and the Slovak Republic) would rank at the top right behind the Czech Republic. Lithuania is not far behind. Second, both countries have maintained liberal foreign trade regimes, which have fostered growth in exports and stimulated efficiency. Here one could argue that currency boards have influenced the policy makers, as the currency board requires free movement of capital, and this naturally presupposes a relatively liberal foreign trade regime. However, having a currency board is naturally not a necessary condition for having a liberal foreign trade regime. For example, Latvia introduced full current account convertibility in June 1994, only a month later than Lithuania.

The favorable development of output in Estonia and Lithuania has not been sufficient to prevent a clear increase in unemployment. Unemployment among the Baltic countries has been the highest in Estonia, where the unemployment rate reached 10 percent in 1995 and has since stayed at approximately the same level. In Lithuania and Latvia the unemployment rate has not been as high, but in 1998–99 and especially during the 1998 financial crisis in Russia unemployment has increased, especially in Latvia. It is of considerable interest to what extent the existing unemployment can be considered structural and can conventional macroeconomic policies reduce the unemployment—obviously a topic for another discussion.

Inflation

The Baltic countries were the fastest among all former Soviet Union countries to reduce inflation. In Estonia inflation is still somewhat higher than in the other two Baltic countries, but there inflation has also recently decreased to single digits. Latvia has had the lowest annual inflation for the past few years. Lately inflation has partly been fueled by the administratively set prices of some commodities in all Baltic countries, as their price increases have been deliberately spread over a prolonged period of time. Inflation in internationally tradable goods has usually been several percentage points lower than headline inflation.

What has the role of the currency board been in reducing inflation in the Baltic countries? We have already seen that in Estonia disinflation was rapid after the introduction of the currency board. This was despite

Table 5.1
Changes in Money Velocity, 1993–97

	Estonia	Latvia	Lithuania	Bulgaria	Czech Republic	Hungary	Poland	Russia
1993	−10.0%			11.7%	30.0%	7.7%	−26.7%	13.1%
1994	12.9%	6.0%	2.9%	19.7%	−27.2%	13.0%	−3.4%	26.0%
1995	4.1%	13.2%	1.3%	12.0%	9.6%	19.5%	0.6%	15.9%
1996	−1.6%	1.3%	23.5%	−9.9%	8.1%	2.3%	−10.6%	7.7%
1997	−1.2%	−17.0%	−14.9%	1.0%	15.0%	−1.0%	−1.8%	−6.1%

the fact that the international reserves of the Bank of Estonia grew, which naturally meant that the monetary base was also growing. Ghosh et al. (1998) found that in countries with currency boards the growth in money was on the average lower than in other countries, but also that those countries had slower growth in the velocity. They termed the effect currency boards have had on the rate of money growth a "discipline effect" and its effects on the velocity a "confidence effect." In Table 5.1 we have calculated the annual changes in velocity and money supply[6] in the Baltic countries and some other transition economies between 1993 and 1997. The changes in money supply are presented in Table 5.2. In Latvia and Lithuania the data starts from 1994, as their national currencies were not introduced until 1993.

The change in velocity is calculated from the identity

$$\Delta v = \Delta p + \Delta y - \Delta m$$

where Δv is the change in velocity, Δp + Δy the change in nominal GDP, and Δm the change in the aforementioned monetary aggregate. Table 5.1 shows first that in Estonia and Lithuania velocity growth has been lower, on the average, than in many other transition economies. It is not surprising that Estonia and Lithuania have had lower velocity growth than countries like Russia and Bulgaria, where inflation has been high and variable during the transition. In Estonia and Lithuania the velocity growth has also been lower than in Hungary and the Czech Republic, which have not experienced episodes of extremely high inflation during the period in question. One should also note Latvia's case. In Latvia the change in velocity is much in line with the experience in the other two countries, so by this criterion the "confidence effect" has been at least as high in Latvia. One can speculate that at least in Latvia this apparent credibility in the currency and by extension monetary pol-

Table 5.2
Changes in Money Supply, 1993–97

	Estonia	Latvia	Lithuania	Bulgaria	Czech Republic	Hungary	Poland	Russia
1993	61.7%			27.9%	−13.0%	11.0%	27.2%	206.9%
1994	18.8%	27.1%	34.8%	41.4%	40.7%	7.7%	33.4%	101.0%
1995	25.5%	0.8%	34.2%	35.0%	6.5%	5.7%	31.0%	79.5%
1996	27.0%	17.2%	3.5%	78.5%	4.6%	18.3%	33.5%	25.0%
1997	20.4%	29.6%	34.4%	227.0%	−7.6%	20.4%	22.2%	22.9%
Average	30.7%	18.7%	26.7%	82.0%	6.2%	12.6%	29.5%	87.1%

Source: International Financial Statistics CD-ROM.

icy has been result of an independent central bank, which has demonstrated its preference for low inflation.[7] The average growth in money supply has been high in both Estonia and Lithuania. In a currency board system large capital inflows translate into growth of the monetary base, which in turn leads to expansion in the larger money aggregates. Here it is interesting to note that Latvia has had a clearly lower growth rate of money than Estonia or Lithuania. In Latvia the central bank has used its power to affect the monetary base and ultimately inflation, but apparently to reach lower inflation, not, for example, to engineer a boost in domestic demand. Here one can also speculate what the effect of the Bank of Latvia's independence has been on monetary policy. Loungani and Sheets (1997) find that central bank independence is negatively correlated with average inflation rate also in the transition economies, a result similar to that of many studies concerning OECD countries. This result persists even after controlling for the stance of fiscal policy and initial conditions.

THE BALTIC CURRENCY BOARDS AND FINANCIAL SYSTEMS

One criticism of currency boards focuses on their inability to function as lenders of last resort if the banking sector should experience liquidity problems. It is at least theoretically possible that this might lead to more volatile development of the banking sector, and perhaps more banking failures than the more conventional central bank model. However, in transition economies the number and scope of banking failures seem to be largely uncorrelated with the type of exchange rate regime chosen, and at least there is no evidence that countries with currency boards have

Table 5.3
Number of Banks at Year-end

	Estonia	Latvia	Lithuania
1992	43	52	27
1993	22	61	27
1994	22	55	27
1995	16	40	16
1996	15		12
1997	12	31	11
1998	6	28	12

Source: Fleming et al. (1996) and national central bank publications.

had more unstable financial systems. In the early stages of transition many banking problems were caused by the outstanding stock of bad debts inherited from the era of the command economy. In addition to this, the new banks were often undercapitalized and did not have the experience necessary to conduct prudent banking operations. Insufficient banking regulations and supervision aggravated the problems. (For an account of the early experiences of bank restructuring in transition economies, see Borish et al. [1995].)

Table 5.3 shows the evolution of the number of banks in the three Baltic countries (including branches of foreign banks). The number of banks has decreased clearly, but most of this decline has been achieved through mergers, not involuntary closures or bank failures. However, banking crises have taken place in all Baltic countries. There were bank closures and recapitalizations by authorities in Estonia in 1992, 1994, and 1998. Lithuania experienced a banking crisis at the end of 1995. The losses to depositors have usually been minimal, except in the Latvian banking crisis of 1995, where the negative net worth of the largest bank was found to be $320 million or approximately 7 percent of GDP. This bank failure was partially caused by a fraud, but also by poor control of currency and interest rate risks (Fleming et al. 1996). It is probably a coincidence that the largest bank failure in the Baltic countries took place in the one Baltic country that did *not* have a currency board in place, but this illustrates well that at least so far many other factors have affected banking systems more than the choice of exchange rate regime.

In its strictest interpretation the currency board system prevents monetary authorities from doing anything when banks are facing difficulties.

In practice the monetary and fiscal authorities in Estonia and Lithuania have been able to intervene when individual banks are in distress. Both in Estonia and Lithuania the central banks have held the currency reserve backing the monetary base well over 100 percent, and this has given them additional leeway in dealing with banking sector problems. According to Fleming et al. (1996) the Estonian monetary authorities have both provided short-term liquidity support (for example, to Social Bank in 1994) and taken over banks and recapitalized them (North Estonian Bank, 1994). In 1998 the Bank of Estonia prompted two small banks to merge and became the majority shareholder in the new bank.

During the Lithuanian banking crisis in 1995 the Bank of Lithuania provided some liquidity support for the first small bank (Aura Bank) to run into difficulties, but as the largest private bank (Innovation Bank) and two other banks were also soon in trouble, the central bank's resources turned out to be inadequate. At this point the Lithuanian parliament passed a law requiring the government to extend guarantees for interbank borrowing by the troubled banks. This illustrates the fact that if the problems in the banking sector are large enough, or truly systemic in nature, in a currency board system the government must step in.

ASSESSING THE BALTIC CURRENCY BOARDS

It is obvious that the Baltic countries have been able to manage the economic transition more successfully than the other former Soviet Union republics. They also appear to be more successful in transition than, for example, Romania and Bulgaria. Initial conditions can explain some of the differences between economic performance, but naturally the policies chosen are also important, and the effects of initial conditions should diminish as more time passes. Consequently, the effect of policies increases.

When one examines the evidence from the different transition economies, it is clear that having a currency board does not produce (or at least has not produced so far) worse economic performance than other exchange rate regimes. Estonia had the smallest output decline of all former Soviet Union countries, and both it and Lithuania have posted high average growth figures after the initial output collapse was halted. However, one can hardly claim that the currency board is a necessary condition for favorable economic development. For example, Poland and Latvia have been able to show reasonably high GDP growth after the transformational recession was over, although in Latvia the resumption of growth was delayed by approximately one year because of the failure of the country's largest bank as well as several smaller ones. (These failures wiped out over one-third of household deposits.)

As is the case with growth, it is hard to argue that having a currency board has been necessary for reducing inflation to low double digits or even single digits in transition economies. Almost all countries in Central and Eastern Europe have managed to keep inflation below 20 percent, and Latvia has recently had the lowest inflation of all transition economies. On the other hand, it is hard to see how Bulgaria could have reduced inflation as successfully as it has done without a currency board and the added credibility it can bring.

If currency boards have not been absolutely necessary for resumption of growth and achieving lower inflation, why have the authorities in different countries implemented them? Why would a monetary authority wish to tie its own hands? There clearly are some costs associated with losing the ability to conduct monetary policy, so what can the benefits be?

Because all Baltic countries are small and open to international trade, conventional analysis would suggest that they would benefit from having a fixed exchange rate. As currency boards are probably the most credible form of fixed exchange rates, perhaps it is not so surprising that they have been adopted in two of the three Baltic countries.

Estonia established its currency board shortly after regaining political independence, as well as after introducing a completely new currency. In these circumstances the currency board was seen as the quickest way to achieve credibility for the currency, and this was what indeed happened. Capital inflows to the country started almost immediately after the introduction of the currency board, and this in a situation where the currency had no history and the new monetary authority no reputation or even experience. Despite all this, the new currency was readily accepted as a medium of exchange (see Lainela and Sutela 1994). Both the inflow of capital and the public's willingness to hold the new currency were clear signs of the credibility of the new currency.

In our opinion, however, the introduction of the currency board was only part of a comprehensive reform package in Estonia. This package was designed to create a stable and predictable macroeconomic environment, to better enable the private sector to function and grow. Another important part of the package was fiscal policy, where the Estonian government has been more or less able to maintain the balance of the central government budget, and even the deficits of the enlarged government have been very small, no more than 1.5 percent of GDP. This reasonably tight fiscal stance has also meant that government has not been in any particular need to finance the deficit from the monetary authorities. On the other hand it could be argued that the fact no such financing was forthcoming has contributed positively to the fiscal restraint. The third part of the package has been the extremely liberal trade policy, which has probably helped to improve efficiency in the economy and promoted exports. As the currency board arrangement is legislatively difficult to change,[8] it may be seen as one cornerstone of this policy package, but its importance should not be overplayed.

Lithuania didn't introduce its national currency litas until August 1993. In Lithuania the decision to introduce the currency board was not unanimous, and the central bank argued against such a move (Lainela and Sutela 1994). Inflation had already been reduced to a reasonably low level, so this was not a case of introducing a currency board in the midst of an economic crisis. Therefore it is interesting to speculate why the currency board was adopted. Part of the reason may have been the success of the Estonian currency board. It had been in operation for over eighteen months and had served Estonia and its economic reforms well. Part of the reason may also have been a genuine desire to solve the time inconsistency problem of the monetary policy. The Lithuanian public sector had a deficit of 3.3 percent of GDP in 1993. In 1994 the deficit grew to 5.5 percent. Introducing a currency board that is not capable of lending to the government removed the temptation to use the central bank to finance the deficit. This deficit financing would have eventually led to higher inflation. Having a currency board forced the public sector to finance its deficit from other, noninflationary sources. Lithuania continued to have high deficits in 1995 and 1996 (4.5 percent of GDP in both years). In this sense the currency board may have prevented high inflation in Lithuania. However, at least *de jure* the Bank of Lithuania is as independent as the Bank of Latvia, so perhaps also the Lithuanian central bank could have attained equally good results concerning inflation without a currency board system.

At the moment Lithuania is in process of giving up the currency board. The Bank of Lithuania has announced that it will give up the currency board and adopt monetary policy based on the more traditional central bank model. The Bank of Lithuania has already introduced some monetary policy instruments, but the litas monetary base is still 100 percent backed by foreign currency reserves. Details of this gradual shift are spelled out in the Bank of Lithuania (1997), which states that Lithuania is giving up the currency board to be better able to react to problems in the financial sector. Other reasons for giving up the currency board include the desire to be able to sterilize capital inflows and generally to influence economic development through monetary policy. In this regard it is interesting that the Bank of Lithuania has announced that they will not give up the system of fixed exchange rates. The litas is still pegged to the US dollar, but by the end of year 2001, it will be pegged to the euro. It remains to be seen whether Lithuania will be as successful as Latvia in maintaining a fixed exchange without a currency board. (One should remember that for approximately the past two years the Bank of Latvia has maintained the ratio of currency reserves to the monetary base at over 100 percent.)

Currency boards in the Baltic (as well as in other) countries have been successfully used in gaining rapid credibility for economic policies (or at least the national currency) in a situation of severe economic turmoil and preventing monetary expansion (and thus inflation) in excess of increase in the foreign currency reserves by committing domestic policy makers to a simple monetary rule.

NOTES

1. Monetary overhang was the result of forced saving during the Soviet era. Households and companies couldn't increase their consumption at the same rate as their money holdings increased. Prices were fixed, and so this excess demand couldn't be eliminated by raising prices, that is, open inflation. On monetary overhang in Russia, see Rautava (1993). For more detailed accounts of the early Russian reforms, see Sutela (1993) and Koen and Marrese (1995).

2. See Hanke et al. (1993).

3. However, there are still some restrictions on foreign buying of real estate.

4. Even though Latvia never had a currency board, we believe it is useful to examine its economic performance as well. It is natural to compare Latvia and its two Baltic neighbors with currency boards, as all three countries are small, are open, and have been parts of the same country for a better part of the twentieth century.

5. There are obvious difficulties in compressing complex economic, social, and legal processes into single numbers, but it is our opinion that these indicators give at least a tolerable picture of the relative ranking of different countries in their progress.

6. We use here the variable *money* from the IMF's International Financial Statistics. This item is equal to the currency outside banks and demand deposits in the banks, that is, it corresponds to M1. For Russia we have used the currency in circulation.

7. See Äimä (1998) for an assessment of the independence of the Baltic central banks. In the case of Estonia and Lithuania, the currency board arrangement requires a great deal of independence for monetary authority, but Latvia seems to be at least as independent as the other two Baltic central banks.

8. Requiring a majority of two-thirds in parliament.

REFERENCES

Äimä, Kustaa. 1998. "Central Bank Independence in the Baltic Countries." *Review of Economies in Transition*. Bank of Finland (April).

Bank of Lithuania. 1997. *Monetary Policy Programme of the Bank of Lithuania for 1997–99*, Resolution no. 14 of the Board of Bank of Lithuania, Vilnius.

Barro, Robert J., and David B. Gordon. 1993. "A Positive Theory of Monetary Policy in a Natural Rate Model." *Journal of Political Economy*, vol. 91, no. 4.

Bennett, Adam G. G. 1992. *The Operation of the Estonian Currency Board*. IMF paper on policy analysis and assessment, no. 92/3.

Borish, Michael S., Millard F. Long, and Michel Noël. 1995. *Restructuring Banks and Enterprises: Recent Lessons from Transition Countries*. World Bank discussion paper, no. 279.

Camard, Wayne. 1996. *Discretion with Rules? Lessons from the Currency Board Arrangement in Lithuania*. IMF paper on policy analysis and assessment, no. 96/1.

European Bank for Restructuring and Development. 1994. *Transition Report*. London.

Fischer, Stanley. 1997. "Closing Remarks: What Have We Learned?" In *Currency Boards and External Shocks: How Much Pain, How Much Gain?* Ed. Guillermo E. Perry. World Bank Latin American and Caribbean Studies, Proceedings Series, Washington, D.C.

Fleming, Alex, Lily Chu, and Marie-Renée Bakker. 1996. *The Baltics—Banking Crises Observed*. Policy Research Working Paper, no. 1647, World Bank, Washington, D.C.

Ghosh, Atish R., Anne-Marie Gulde, and Holger C. Wolf. 1998. *Currency Boards: The Ultimate Fix?* IMF working paper, no. 98/8.

Gomulka, Stanislaw. 1998. "Output: Causes of the Decline and the Recovery." In *Emerging from Communism*. Eds. Peter Boone, Stanislaw Gomulka, and Richard Layard. Cambridge, Mass: The MIT Press.

Hanke, Steve H., Lars Jonung, and Kurt Schuler. 1993. *Estonia: It's Not a Currency Board!* Transition no. 1.

Havrylyshyn, Oleh, Ivailo Izvorski, and Ron van Rooden. 1998. *Recovery and Growth in Transition Economies 1990–1997: A Stylized Regression Analysis*. IMF working paper, no. 98/141.

Honohan, Patrick. 1994. *Currency Board or Central Bank? Lessons from the Irish Pound's Link with Sterling, 1928–79*. Centre for Economic Policy Research discussion paper, no. 1040.

Isard, Peter. 1995. *Exchange Rate Economics*. Cambridge: Cambridge University Press.

Koen, Vincent, and Michael Marrese. 1995. "Stabilization and Structural Change in Russia, 1992–1994." In *Road Maps of the Transition*. Ed. Banerjee, Bigwajit, et al. IMF occasional paper, no. 127.

Korhonen, Iikka. 1996. "Banking Sectors in Baltic Countries." *Review of Economies in Transition*. Bank of Finland (April).

Korhonen, Iikka, Toivo Kuus, and Villu Zirnask. 2000 forthcoming. *Baltic Securities Market*, in *Journal of Baltic Studies*.

Kwan, Yum K., and Francis T. Liu. 1996. *Hong Kong's Currency Board and Changing Monetary Regimes*. NBER working paper, no. 5723.

Lainela, Seija, and Pekka Sutela. 1994. *The Baltic Economies in Transition*. Bank of Finland A:91. Helsinki.

Loungani, Prakash, and Nathan Sheets. 1997. "Central Bank Independence, Inflation, and Growth in Transition Economies." *Journal of Money, Credit, and Banking*, vol. 29, no. 3 (August).

Mundell, Robert A. 1961. "A Theory of Optimum Currency Areas." *American Economic Review* 51.

Rautava, Jouko. 1993. "Monetary Overhang, Inflation and Stabilization in the Economies in Transition." *Review of Economies in Transition*. Bank of Finland (April).

Santiprabhob, Veerathai. 1997. *Bank Soundness and Currency Board Arrangements: Issues and Experience*. IMF paper on policy analysis and assessment, no. 97/11.

Sutela, Pekka. 1993. "Overview." In *The Russian Economy in Crisis and Transition*. Ed. Pekka Sutela. Bank of Finland A:86.

Williamson, John. 1995. *What Role for Currency Boards?* Washington, D.C.: Institute for International Economics.

6

The Currency Board in Estonia

Mart Sörg and Vello Vensel

As discussed in Chapters 3, 4, and 5, a number of countries have established currency board arrangements in recent years. The IMF staff has discussed the introduction of currency board arrangements with postconflict Somalia and Liberia. In some cases a currency board arrangement has been a major element of a stabilization program (Currency Board Arrangement 1997, p. 54). In the opinion of researchers and politicians in several countries, a stable currency based on a currency board arrangement is a cornerstone of the success of Estonian economic reform. For example, during his visit to the country in May 1994, George Soros stated already then that Estonia's success is based on a stable and convertible monetary unit, the Estonian kroon (Kalda 1994, p. 25).

Currency boards are not a new phenomenon in economics. In addition to the discussion in Chapters 3, 4, and 5, it should be noted here that the currency board principle was established in the Bank Charter Act of 1844, where the Issue Department of the Bank of England acted as a currency board. For this reason, many of the British colonies in Africa, Asia, and the Caribbean used currency boards upon introduction of their own currencies. More than seventy such boards operated at one time. Among the best known examples of territories that still have a currency board of some kind are Hong Kong and Singapore. There is also voluminous literature about the experience of the currency board arrangement in various countries (see Balino and Enoch 1997; Enoch and Gulde 1997; Eichengreen et al. 1998; Ghosh et al. 1998).

The orthodox currency board is not subordinate to a central bank but backs bank notes with foreign assets. Therefore, some observers do not consider present-day currency board arrangements to be real currency boards (Hanke, Jonung, and Schuler 1993, p. 12). However, as the main characteristic of a currency board is its requirement to exchange domestic currency for a foreign reserve currency at a fixed rate, it may be concluded that Estonia does have a currency board arrangement that conforms to present-day developments in money and central banking, as did the orthodox currency board in its own time.

The liberation of the CEEC from the socialist political and economic regime previously forced on them, gave birth to financial and economic problems analogous to those caused by the liberation from colonial subjection. It was therefore natural for the idea of the currency board to be reborn in the 1990s. The aim of a currency board system is to achieve currency convertibility and a fixed exchange rate, and thereby help to stabilize the economy, bring about structural change, and integrate the country into the world economy as quickly as possible.

Estonia has had seven years of positive experience in applying a currency board system, which permits some generalizations about its positive and negative impacts on the development of the country's economic reforms. Given the spread of the currency board arrangement, the time seems right for trying to draw some conclusions about its performance at the present time. The currency board seems to be fulfilling its objectives. By choosing the external discipline of a currency board arrangement, the government has enhanced the credibility of its intentions to fight inflation, and policy makers operate within a relatively predictable internal monetary environment.

This chapter attempts this assessment by drawing on the Estonian case. The remainder of the chapter is organized as follows. Historical notes about the necessity of a currency reform in Estonia in 1992 are presented in the second section. The advantages of a fixed exchange rate regime in a small transition economy are discussed in the third section. Estonian monetary system main characteristics are presented in the fourth section, and the impact of the monetary system on the Estonian economy in the fifth section. Some future prospects of the Estonian currency board arrangement are presented in the sixth section, and the chapter ends with some conclusions.

NECESSITY OF A CURRENCY REFORM: HISTORICAL NOTES

In August 1991 the three Baltic states regained their independence from the Soviet Union, and Estonia was the first to introduce its own currency—the Estonian kroon (EEK)—in June 1992. The idea that Estonia should have its own currency dates from September 1987, when four Estonian social scientists put forward a proposal for Estonian economic autonomy. The supporters of the idea of a national monetary system hoped to achieve three objectives: (1) eliminate inflationary influences from the East—Russia and the former Soviet republics, (2) establish an approximate macroeconomic balance of supply and demand, and (3) conquer persistent cash crises (Kallas and Sörg 1995, p. 53).

Hyperinflation had broken out due to the liberalization of prices and the disruption of Estonia's trade with the former Soviet Union at the beginning of 1992. The consumer price index rose by 87 percent in January 1992, 74 percent in February, and 30 percent in March in comparison with the previous month. This caused sharp cash crises and threatened to paralyze monetary circulation completely. The Bank of Estonia and the Estonian Savings Bank issued checkbooks (a major innovation) to alleviate the shortage of cash but the population used them reluctantly. The public sector was instructed to pay wages four times a month, instead of twice as previously, and a ceiling on cash payments was fixed at 1,000 rubles. Permission was given to use foreign currency alongside the ruble in buying and selling goods and services.

Various means of payment started to emerge spontaneously in enterprises, which were used for shopping there, and on March 25, 1992, the board of the Bank of Estonia gave permission for the introduction of temporary money in Tartu—so-called Tartu currency—to alleviate the shortage of cash (Kallas and Sörg 1995, p. 57). Confidence in the inflationary ruble, also called the "occupation ruble," was lost completely. This was stressed by a higher dollarization ratio than elsewhere in the Baltic states.

Before Estonia's currency reform (second quarter of 1992) the dollarization ratio peaked around 60 percent in Estonia, 50 percent in Lithuania (first quarter of 1993), and 35 percent in Latvia (first quarter of 1993) (Sahay and Végh 1995, p. 37). For the Estonian authorities such a situation set up two conditions for a successful currency reform: (1) the currency reform had to be carried out as quickly as possible before multiple

Table 6.1
Changes in the CPI, 1992 (compared with the previous month, %)

	General Index	Food	Manufactured Goods	Services
January	87.0	118.5	40.5	58.6
February	74.0	72.1	64.1	135.7
March	30.0	14.5	52.8	88.8
April	10.6	4.4	25.4	5.8
May	5.2	−0.3	7.6	25.8
June	11.4	7.9	16.3	12.6
July	24.3	25.2	16.3	40.8
August	17.6	12.8	32.4	8.4
September	6.6	3.1	5.1	18.4
October	7.7	1.1	14.0	11.3
November	9.5	20.6	0.1	8.6
December	3.3	5.2	1.2	3.1

Source: Sörg 1994, p.180.

wage and inflation shocks caused a social explosion and economic collapse, and (2) the new currency had to inspire confidence, although introduced under circumstances of deep economic crisis and lack of experience by the central bank in carrying out monetary policy.

An early goal of monetary reform was to control inflation. However, during the first month after the currency reform, prices rose sharply (Table 6.1), which can be interpreted as a temporary effect of the currency reform. The rise in prices was mostly the effect of merging two goods markets (foreign currency shops and ruble shops) and eliminating the cash shortage experienced by the population of Estonia. Hence, during the first month after the currency reform, the cash in circulation doubled. Another reason was higher tax rates in order to balance the central government budget (the value added tax, or VAT, rose from 10 to 18 percent).

Those who carry out a currency reform must take into account a temporary acceleration of inflation. Having eliminated the shortage of cash, it is necessary to create confidence in the new currency. This may be done by means of a currency board arrangement, where the value of the new currency is fixed in terms of a major reserve currency. In Estonia the exchange rate between the kroon (EEK) and the mark (DM) was based on the prevailing market exchange rate between the Soviet ruble

(SUR) and the DM, approximately 80 SUR= 1 DM. Rubles were thus exchanged for kroons at the rate 10 SUR = 1 EEK, and the Estonian exchange rate was fixed at 8 EEK = 1 DM. Seeing that this rate took into account the gloomy future of the ruble, the kroon was undervalued by 4 to 5 times. According to UN data, the price level in Estonia in 1993 was 4 times lower than in Austria if the official exchange rate between EEK and the Austrian schilling is taken as a basis. The undervaluation was obviously too big and caused inflationary pressure on consumer prices. However, the inflation rate in Estonia declined continuously (Table 6.2) and in 1998 the consumer price index increase had reached a level lower than 10 percent.

A moderate inflation rate (up to 10 to 15 percent) is useful to a transition economy for several reasons: (1) it is easier to adjust the wage and price structure derived from the old socialist system and unsuitable for a market economy upward instead of correcting the components equally upward and downward by subtracting from the one and adding to the other; (2) it is impossible to enforce sufficiently high tax rates given the weakness of public authorities and the low living standard of the population, and inflation tax helps to balance the state less painfully; and (3) inflation causes the real value (purchasing power) of bank deposits to decline continuously, and money is redistributed among its more active users. This causes primary capital accumulation to take place and facilitates the rapid development of a new type of entrepreneurship.

THE ADVANTAGES OF A FIXED EXCHANGE RATE IN A TRANSITION ECONOMY

In 1991–92 the Estonian political elite had already come to the decision that a liberal economic policy would be best for the country. The then prime minister of Estonia, Mart Laar (who, by the way, is from March 1999 once again the prime minister of Estonia), stressed the following in his address at a colloquium of the German Foreign Policy Association in June 1993: "A vital factor in Estonia's economic success has been the openness of the Estonian economy" (Laar 1993). Estonia introduced liberal economic policy. Besides the smallness of the Estonian market there are other reasons for this too:

1. the long-term experience of the overregulated socialist command economy had been strongly unfavorable and thus gave rise to a generally negative attitude toward state regulation

Table 6.2
Inflation Compared to the Previous Year (%)

	1992	1993	1994	1995	1996	1997	1998
Increase in consumer prices (CPI)	1076.5	89.8	47.7	29.0	23.1	11.2	8.2
Open sector	991.6	84.9	33.9	17.5	18.6	7.8	6.4
Sheltered sector	1702.7	149.3	89.2	52.1	30.5	15.8	13.4
Increase in producer prices (PPI)	—	99.9	36.8	25.6	14.9	8.9	3.9
Increase in export prices	—	—	—	15.1	11.3	7.5	2.1

Source: Bank of Estonia.

2. regulation demands financial resources, but in a transition economy there is a lack of money even for the most urgent social and other government expenditures
3. public authorities were weak both politically and economically. For a long time the population had regarded the state as the instrument of a foreign power and passive resistance to government structures was widespread. If the authorities in the restored Estonian republic had tried to impose significantly higher tax rates than before and tighter regulation, the reaction to these measures would have been hostile—and more. Events in other postsocialist countries have also shown that the more liberal the economic policy of a country is, the faster the improvements caused by reforms will work to stop the decline of the economy. In order to prevent the development of pressures that might be conducive to a return to the former system, the first stage of transition (economic decline) must be passed as quickly as possible.

The market economy has proved a flexible and robust system of organizing production in a modern society. For a market economy to function efficiently, at least three things must be in place: private ownership, free competition and exchange of goods, and a "hard" budget constraint that permits bankruptcy and thus creates the conditions necessary for economic renewal and growth (Isachen, Hamilton, and Gulfason 1994, p. 127). It follows from these principles that the market economy also needs a currency in which people will have confidence. While the Estonian economy, reorienting itself to a new economic system and new markets, was passing through a deep crisis, it was difficult to forecast the behavior of the market. The central bank lacked experience in how to manage the money supply. There was not even a theory of economic transition from socialism to capitalism and the only way to have a currency that inspired confidence was to introduce a fixed exchange rate. This had been clear long before the currency reform itself. The ideas of a stable currency and free convertibility have indeed been reflected in the Estonian monetary system and monetary policy.

The Estonian monetary system is considered particularly liberal because the kroon's purchasing power and currency flows are entirely determined by market forces and there is convertibility on both the current and the capital account. No restrictions are imposed on the flows of currency and capital to and from Estonia. It is also possible in Estonia to freely convert foreign currency into Estonian kroons and vice versa, and to hold one's savings in either foreign currency or the kroon. No maximum or minimum rates of interests on deposits and loans have been imposed. In addition, the right of people to hold and use their money is secured by the fact that its stability is guaranteed by pegging the Estonian kroon to the mark at the fixed exchange rate of 8 to 1, and the currency in circulation is (at least) 100 percent backed by foreign reserves. Estonian banks are liquid and there are enough currency exchange offices—more than 500 for a population of 1.5 million. In addition, banks use electronic credit cards and electronic payment systems. All these attributes secure the operational use of money.

Liberal monetary policy goes together well with the main objective of Estonia's reform policy, which is developing a free and open economy. The positive influence of liberal monetary policy on economic reform in Estonia becomes significant when it is realized that an illiberal monetary policy would, at least to an extent, have sustained the old structures and customs and thus hindered the birth of market forces.

The major reason why orthodox monetary policy might have failed in Estonia or not have been introduced in the first place was the weakness of state power and the habit of civil servants and the population to ignore laws and regulations. If measures to enforce control had been taken, this would only have deepened the rift between the introduction and application of state economic policy (including the monetary policy). This is, for example, illustrated by the accusation that the Bank of Estonia (BOE) robbed pensioners of their "funeral money" in the 1992 monetary reform, which can still be heard, although all ruble bank deposits were exchanged at the same exchange rate that applied to prices and pensions. Thus, the currency reform only made it clear to depositors that due to inflation, their savings had lost most of their value (purchasing power).

Another reason for adopting liberal monetary policy was the absence of the necessary conditions and means to manage the monetary demand and supply. At the end of 1990 the equity capital of the Bank of Estonia was only 10 million rubles and it had to borrow 6 million rubles from the Estonian Insurance Agency. In 1991, when domestic currency had to be printed abroad, the BOE postponed issuing a letter of credit to the printers because it had not received the necessary hard currency ($2 million) from the government. The amount of reserve currency necessary to back the kroon issue during the 1992 currency reform was U.S. $120 million, which was also not achieved on time. On July 16, 1992, nearly a month after the currency reform, the BOE published its first balance sheet, which showed foreign exchange reserves of EEK 1,165 million ($98 million). In the draft of the 1992 annual report, the BOE gold and foreign currency reserves were, on June 30, 1992, said to be only EEK 718 million ($57.9 million).

Introducing a fixed exchange rate regime during the period of transition first of all allowed the central bank to minimize the wrong decisions that it might have made due to the lack of theory, information, skill, and experience. The Estonian statistics system was, and still is, in a process of evolution. Gathering initial data is complicated and in the circumstances of economic transition, it is not possible to determine and assess long-term trends. Preliminary data are unreliable and often late. For example, the Statistical Office published exact GDP data for 1993 only at the beginning of February 1995. According to presently available sources, Estonia's GDP decreased between 8.5 and 9.0 percent in 1993. In May 1994, however, the Statistical Office recorded a 7.8 percent decline. The IMF again showed a 3 percent decline.

The Bank of Estonia in turn published the most optimistic figures, showing a 3 percent positive GNP growth in 1993 (Lainela and Sutela 1994, p. 21). If the last-mentioned estimate had been accepted, then the wrong monetary policy might easily have been followed. From the above example it is clear that the central authorities cannot manage the economy efficiently until there are reliable theories about the influence of monetary policy in a transition economy. Consequently, until then, the market should be allowed to find the right path. The risk of bad decisions is aggravated by a high level of corruption and the influence of corporate personalities on public authorities in transition economies including in Estonia.

The authors are of the opinion now, that when there is a need for

Table 6.3
Foreign Investment in Central and Eastern European Countries (in U.S. $ millions)

Country	1992	1993	1994	Per Capita in 1989–94	Per Capita in 1994
Czech Republic	983	517	850	289	83
Estonia	58	160	253	295	158
Hungary	1471	2339	1146	671	111
Latvia	43	51	155	92	57
Lithuania	27	61	60	46	16
Poland	284	580	542	40	14
Russia	700	400	1000	11	7
Slovakia	100	156	187	84	35

Source: EBRD Transition Report 1994.

Estonian exporters to raise their competitiveness, something that domestic inflation forces these firms to do all the time, they strive to improve quality, reduce costs, and look for new markets and products. Here the fixed exchange rate remains the most impartial judge in the market. Fluctuations in the kroon's exchange rate would create undeserved advantages for some and equally undeserved disadvantages for others (e.g., the users of imported raw materials). The share of intermediate goods sent to Estonia to be processed has grown rapidly. While they accounted for 14 percent of overall export turnover in 1994, in 1997 the respective figure was almost 27 percent. In 1997, the exports of processed goods formed 71 percent of total machinery exports, while the relative share of clothing was 46 percent of manufacturing exports. In 1998, the real growth of exports was 16 percent while the growth rate of the reexport of imported for manufacturing goods was about 40 percent.

It may be noted that foreign investors are careful in placing their money in countries with an economy-in-transition. Moreover, in 1992–94 international stock market transactions had not yet materialized in Estonia. A fixed exchange rate coupled with a liberal monetary policy was therefore no less than an essential precondition for foreign investors to risk putting their capital in Estonia. At first, foreign capital came in small amounts, but by 1994 Estonia was well-known enough and outstripped the other transitional CEEC in respect of foreign investment per capita (Table 6.3).

Foreign direct investment into Estonia continued to rise during the years 1995–98 (see Tables 6.9 and 6.14). There was a danger that Asian and Russian crises could affect the prospects of foreign direct investment in Estonia and other Eastern and Central European transition economies negatively. Sharp falls in equity prices and foreign exchange rates in these markets made their assets considerably cheaper and created new opportunities for foreign investments.

But there was also the possibility that political stability and liberalization measures were not enough to attract foreign investment, especially in Russia. Foreign direct investments in the Baltic states, including Estonia, continued to grow rapidly. By FDI inflow per capita, Estonia is one of the leading Central and Eastern European transition countries (in 1997, U.S. $183); also remarkable is the ratio of FDI to GDP—5.7 percent in 1997. In 1998, FDI inflow into Estonia even increased and the ratio of FDI to GDP was as high as 10.8 percent. The overall amount of FDI into Estonia has grown to 24.2 million kroons for the beginning of 1999.

ESTONIAN MONETARY SYSTEM: MAIN CHARACTERISTICS

In May 1992 the Estonian parliament (Riigikogu) passed three laws: the Currency Law, the Law of Backing the Estonian Kroon, and the Foreign Currency Law. These laws were, however, not applied at once but from the moment when the monetary reform came into force. These laws lay down the principles of Estonia's currency and monetary system. They make the operation of the Estonian currency board the task of the central bank, which also retains the option of pursuing certain monetary policies.

In order to allow the currency board to operate efficiently, it was deemed necessary to safeguard the independence of the Bank of Estonia to a large extent, while regulating its detailed functions as a currency board. The independence of the Bank of Estonia is guaranteed by the following stipulations: it is not allowed to extend credit to the government, its assets are kept separate from the state budget, and its managerial staff is appointed by Estonia's president and parliament. The Bank of Estonia has been instructed that the exchange rate of the kroon is fixed (or pegged) nominally to the mark (1DM = 8EEK). Only parliament can change this nominal anchor, although the Bank of Estonia may permit fluctuations of the pegged rate within margins of 3 percent.

The decree of the Estonian currency reform committee, "On the Per-

Table 6.4
Key Monetary Data (in million kroons, at the end of a month)

	Cash Issued by BOE	Accounts of Commercial Banks Held with BOE	Gold and Foreign Reserves of BOE	Purchasing Power of Kroon in Domestic Market 06/92 = 1.000
06/92	365.5	245.5	1165.2	1.000
07/92	677.7	317.9	1541.2	0.816
08/92	781.5	420.2	1635.6	0.677
09/92	874.2	309.6	1607.0	0.635
10/92	973.5	517.6	2023.1	0.590
11/92	1084.6	556.6	2213.3	0.538
12/92	1228.6	580.5	2370.4	0.521

Source: Bank of Estonia.

formance of Currency Reform," dated June 17, 1992, provided the main features of the currency reform. The decree established the Estonian kroon as the sole legal tender in the republic of Estonia, going into effect at 4 A.M. on June 20, 1992. It also determined that every resident whose name was on an approved list could exchange up to 1,500 rubles, one-off, between June 20 and 22 at the rate 10 rubles = 1 kroon. Rubles exceeding this sum could be converted into kroons in unlimited quantities at the exchange rate 50:1, until July 1, 1992. In addition to the 1,500 rubles in cash, residents could exchange cash checks, demand and time deposits with the banks, as well as deposit certificates of the Bank of Estonia at the exchange rate 10:1. A total of 768.4 million rubles in cash deposited with banks was removed from circulation by the currency reform, and 1,567.5 million rubles were accepted from residents at cash exchange offices. A total of EEK 157 million in cash was thus supplied to 1.1 million residents by means of currency exchange, and ruble deposits were converted into kroons to the extent of EEK 207 million. Thus every resident exchanged the equivalent sum of DM 28 on the average (Kallas and Sörg 1995, p. 59).

Seeing that the Currency Law allowed only the kroon as quid pro quo in the exchange process, the demand for kroon notes in circulation increased. The supply of bank money also increased, due to the fact that there was no need for barter transactions anymore, and also because of the high inflation rate at the time. This can be seen in Table 6.4.

As the currency board determined the kroons in circulation to be fully

Table 6.5
Dynamics of Relocation of Monetary Resources in Estonia (in million kroons)

	June 30, 1992	December 31, 1992	December 31, 1993	December 31, 1997	December 31, 1998
Gold and foreign currency reserves of the BOE	718	2502	5237	10902	10908
Cash in circulation	366	1229	2730	5352	5391
Reserves of commercial banks in the BOE	370	581	1147	2514	3658
Total assets of commercial banks	6256	4788	6396	38755	40994
Convertible currency accounts of commercial banks	1911	874	280	16521	15506

Source: Bank of Estonia.

covered by gold and foreign reserves, then the main way of buying cash kroons was to sell foreign currency to the Bank of Estonia. This was the reason why the foreign exchange in circulation and held by the banks began to flow to the Bank of Estonia. It is evident from Table 6.5 that immediately after the currency reform, the gold and foreign currency reserves of the BOE were significantly less than those of the commercial banks, but by the end of 1993 the foreign currency reserves of the BOE exceeded those of the commercial banks by more than 18 times. Obviously a decrease in the population's hard currency holdings contributed to this development.

After the currency reform the population's cash in hard currencies was replaced by Estonian kroons. By July 1, 1992, kroons were 18.5 percent of money in circulation (M2D), and by August 1, 1992, it had risen to 29.6 percent. At first the relative share of cash in the total money supply (in kroons) was 30 percent. The increment of cash has slowed down over time. Thus, Table 6.6 shows that the monthly increase in cash was highest in 1992, after which it has been decreasing from year to year, and in 1998 there was even negative increment of issued cash.

As the Estonian kroon received a warm welcome by the population and business enterprises alike, the Foreign Currency Law was of no use anymore. This law had come into force with the currency reform and provided that foreign currency be used only in clearing accounts with

Table 6.6
Additionally Issued Cash (in million kroons)

Year	Per Annum	Per Month (average)
1992 (June 20–Dec. 31)	862.7	136.9
1993	1501.6	125.1
1994	769.3	64.1
1995	824.8	68.7
1996	649.6	54.1
1997	541.8	45.2
1998	−96.1	−8.0

Source: Bank of Estonia.

foreign countries, and that the bank rendering this service must have the necessary license from the central bank. To concentrate foreign currency reserves at the central bank and thus increase the kroon's reserve assets, legal persons were required to sell their assets in foreign currency within two months through an intermediary bank to the BOE. Government bodies and institutions had to do so within seven days.

In order not to disturb external economic activity, importers could buy foreign exchange without restriction. It was enacted that individuals and legal persons could not have foreign currency accounts in Estonia, and all foreign currency paid to them had to be converted into kroons. As it soon became evident that foreign currencies would not drive the Estonian kroon out of circulation, and in order to simplify business, the board of the BOE on July 8, 1992, permitted large-scale enterprises with a high share of foreign trade to have foreign currency accounts abroad. As the Estonian kroon repeatedly proved its vitality, the restrictions in the Foreign Currency Law were gradually reduced and in March 1994 parliament annulled the law completely.

The openness of the Estonian monetary system is guaranteed by the free inflow and outflow of foreign currency. The exchange of the formerly inconvertible currencies of the (ex-Soviet) CIS countries is now also allowed. The Bank of Estonia daily fixes the exchange rates between the kroon and major foreign currencies. For a long time the rate was determined as a ratio to the currencies of twenty industrial countries, but in February 1997, thirteen other currencies (those of Kazakhstan, Greece, Lithuania, Latvia, Moldova, Portugal, the Czech Republic, Ukraine, Hungary, Uzbekistan, New Zealand, Belarus, Russia) were added to the list.

Table 6.7
Estonian Foreign Trade after the Currency Reform in 1992 (in million kroons)

	Exports		Imports		Trade Balance
	Total	*Incl. West*	*Total*	*Incl. West*	
May	340	198	308	210	32
June	381	244	359	227	22
July	698	376	587	380	111
August	568	322	513	309	55
September	601	343	594	326	7
October	573	339	633	405	−60
November	546	353	536	286	10
December	655	433	588	361	67

Source: Bank of Estonia.

At the end of 1997 the assets and liabilities of banks in foreign currencies were 44.0 percent and 42.6 percent of their respective totals; at the end of 1998, correspondingly 54.6 percent and 37.8 percent. The major currencies concerned are the DM and USD, and at the end of 1998 they formed about 95 percent of the banks' total foreign currency assets and liabilities.

IMPACT OF THE MONETARY SYSTEM ON THE ECONOMY

Before the currency reform, shops in Estonia had been practically empty and basic consumer goods were subject to rationing cards. A major achievement of the currency reform was to end the shortage economy. The most important reason for this was undoubtedly the restoration of the propensity to save. Despite negative real interest rates, the savings of the population steadily increased during the postreform period. The increase in time deposits was especially rapid. At the end of June 1992 time deposits formed 4.1 percent of total kroon deposits; at the end of October 1992 the figure was already 10.6 percent.

The incentive to produce and to import Western goods was also highly motivated by the stable currency relation. The impact was significantly expressed by the growth of both export and import capacities (Table 6.7).

Due to the fact that consumer prices in Estonia's limited internal market have been rising in comparison with the prices of its Western business partners, Western imports have become more and more profitable and attractive, and since 1993 Estonia's trade balance has continuously been negative. The major part of the deficit derives from Western trade. In 1998 imports into Estonia amounted to 53,502 million kroons (in 1992 it was EEK 5,128 million) while exports were 37,779 million kroons (EEK 5,549 million in 1992). Thus the volume of foreign trade has grown rapidly and exceeds Estonia's nominal GDP to a significant extent—in 1998 about 1.25 times (estimated GDP in 1998 was about 73.2 billion kroons).

The Currency Law ended the (Soviet-type) system of hard currency shops, and all goods are now sold for Estonian kroons. Thus, imported goods became available to everybody but, contrary to expectations, the sales of imported goods declined considerably in the first postreform weeks because of the great difference between the prices of imported and domestic goods. As a consequence, the prices of domestic goods rose and those of imported goods fell. The reaction was sharp: while a Gallup poll in the first half of 1992 revealed unsatisfied net consumer demand, a similar poll in the third quarter of the same year showed that 19 percent of shop assistants thought they could now meet the demand (Kallas and Sörg 1995, p. 66).

The big success of the currency board system has been to abate inflation. The rate of inflation had dropped somewhat just before the currency reform, but after the reform there was a great jump upward again. The original rise was caused by an increase in taxes ensuing from the currency reform and further price liberalization. In the foreseeable future, an inflation rate of about 10 percent will probably be normal despite the peg of the kroon to the mark. The reason is the lag of domestic prices and especially wage levels vis-à-vis the European levels. The average monthly wage in Estonia was 4,100 kroons (DM 512, taxes included) in 1998. Yet in Estonia the rise in prices has been on the same level (or even less) than in the other postsocialist countries. The liberalization of prices in 1992 increased the kroon's real exchange rate index in relation to Estonia's Eastern trading partners more than 2.3 times, but at the end of October 1997 the index had dropped to 0.837, and then raised again (see Table 6.8). In February 1999, it was less than 1.0 in trading with Lithuania (0.599) and with Latvia (0.836).

Research by the IMF has shown that countries with a currency peg have comparatively low inflation. For example, in a sample of countries, those with pegged exchange rates had an average annual inflation rate

Table 6.8
Estonian Real Exchange Rate Index (June 1992 = 1)

	Index	Western Trading Partners	Eastern Trading Partners
10/92	1.991	1.830	2.320
10/93	1.900	2.778	0.957
10/94	2.430	3.770	1.097
10/95	2.658	4.776	0.899
10/96	2.891	5.391	0.900
10/97	3.015	5.923	0.837
10/98	3.666	6.579	1.265
02/99	3.576	6.467	1.209

Source: Bank of Estonia.

of 8 percent, compared with 14 percent for intermediate and 16 percent for floating exchange rate systems (Ghosh, Guelde, Ostry, and Wolf 1996, p. 4).

It has been theoretically argued that exchange rate volatility adds to business cost and risk (Langmore 1995, p. 189). In Estonia, from time to time, there are rumors about an impending devaluation or revaluation of the kroon. Banks have increasingly begun to write into loan contracts clauses that would ensure them against losses caused by a change in the kroon exchange rate; also, the number of derivative contracts is rising. This shows that there are enough persons who are against the fixed exchange rate. However, it is only due to the currency board system and a liberal monetary policy that foreign investors have agreed to invest their money in Estonia. This applies particularly to long-term investments. For example, in 1997 about 70 percent of the foreign investments in Estonia were made in industry and transport, storage, and communications, and in 1998 53.8 percent in the financial sector (see Table 6.9).

On June 3, 1996, the Tallinn Stock Exchange was inaugurated as an electronic share market. Transactions are carried out via the Estonian Central Depository for Securities Ltd., founded in February 1994. The opening of the stock exchange brought about a rapid growth in market liquidity and the rate of portfolio investment. In 1996 the capacity of the capital market in Estonia increased approximately 4 times and by the end of the year had reached 13.2 billion kroons, which forms 28 percent of the GDP. This is said to exceed comparative figures in all the states

Table 6.9
Foreign Direct Investments by Kind of Activity, 1997 and 1998 (in million kroons and %)

Spheres of Activities	1997	1998
Industry	1293 (35.6%)	1509 (19.0%)
Transport, storage and communications	902 (24.9%)	—
Wholesale and retail trade	325 (9.0%)	—
Finance	575 (15.9%)	4269 (53.8%)
Real estate, leasing and business activities	170 (4.7%)	385 (4.8%)
Other	362 (9.9%)	1779 (22.4%)
Total	3627 (100.0%)	7942 (100%)

Source: Bank of Estonia.

of the CEEC, except the Czech Republic. In March 1997 the Tallinn exchange exceeded the daily turnovers of the Riga and Lithuanian stock exchanges on the average of 5 to 6 times. By the end of 1996 the volume index of the Tallinn Central Depository for Securities (TALSE) had increased about 5 times within a year-and-a-half. The growing interest of foreign investors in the Estonian capital market has been of great advantage in this context (Table 6.10).

The authors completely agree with Stanley Fischer that the currency board system is the strongest form of commitment to a fixed exchange rate, although its gold standard-type monetary policy rules may put severe strain on the banking system. A currency board can work well if fiscal policy is highly responsible—or becomes so as a result of the currency board—and if the commercial banks operate on an international scale (Fischer 1996, p. 37). Estonia's balance of payments has in fact been sufficiently balanced, because the current account deficit is compensated by the inflow of foreign capital due to a favorable investment climate.

A currency board not only demands the internationalization of commercial banks, but creates favorable conditions for it by the low exchange rate risk. At the end of 1998, 58 percent of the stock of Estonian commercial banks was held by foreign owners (in 1997, 43 percent), and the shares of the two major banks are quoted on the Frankfurt and Helsinki exchanges. Estonian banks have acquired or, are about to acquire, banks in the other Baltic states and the republics of the CIS. Also, the number of international bank cards and their use are growing rapidly (Table 6.11).

Table 6.10
Characteristics of the Estonian Capital Market, 1995–98

Characteristics	1995	1996	1997	1998
1. Market Capitalization (in billion kroons)	3.2	13.4	24.5	15.1
2. Share of Issuers (%):				
Companies	90.6	87.3	93.5	89.4
Public Sector	6.3	9.0	4.9	6.6
Nonresidents	3.1	3.7	1.6	4.0
3. Share of Investors (%):				
Residents	68.8	64.9	61.2	62.9
—among this institutional investors	59.4	56.0	50.2	54.3
Nonresidents	31.2	35.1	38.8	37.1
4. Share of Instruments (%):				
Shares	68.8	78.4	77.1	71.5
Obligations	28.1	17.2	16.3	24.5
Others	3.1	4.4	6.6	4.0
5. Turnover (in billion kroons)	0.01	4.1	34.1	33.7
6. Turnover of the Stock Exchange	—	2.3	22.0	13.4
7. Capitalization/GDP (%)	8	26	39	20
8. Turnover/Capitalization (%)	3	31	139	226

Source: Bank of Estonia; author's calculations.

And to summarize briefly: the major advantages of currency boards are: (1) they issue a medium of exchange to facilitate trade and other transactions; (2) the local currency they issue provides a satisfactory unit of account; (3) the currency issued by the boards promotes the financial confidence necessary for the growth of the economy (Ghatak 1995, p. 73). In the case of Estonia these advantages have paved the way for the success of its economic reforms.

However, the experience of currency boards in postcolonial Africa points to the weaknesses of the system. The chief criticisms of currency boards can be summarized as follows: (1) Since the volume of currency is linked to the state of the balance of payments, the supply of money is reduced whenever the balance of payments is negative. In other words, the economy has to deflate at the time of a deficit on the balance of payments. Contrariwise, with a surplus on the balance of payments, the

Table 6.11
Number of Bank Cards and Terminal Centers in Estonia (end of year; unit)

	1994	1995	1996	1997	1998
Domestic bank cards	5000	108200	381300	406200	292345
International debit cards	—	9000	42700	186300	386118
International credit cards	—	2300	9300	14900	19163
Bank cards total	5000	119500	433300	607400	697626
Automatic teller machines	5	140	230	427	490
Points of sale accepting bank cards	20	250	1200	2153	2586

Source: Bank of Estonia.

money supply expands. (2) Domestic finance is thus really governed by the vagaries of foreign trade and such a situation may be considered unacceptable. (3) The financial system will fail to promote the growth of poor regions since it is not designed to perform this function. (4) The existence of a currency board deprives a country of monetary sovereignty, which would be needed to pursue independent economic policies. (5) Currency boards have also been criticized because of the cost of the foreign reserves necessary to back the local currency (Ghatak 1995, pp. 73–74).

In the Estonian case these problems are not acute because the negative trade balance has been offset by capital inflow; Estonian monetary sovereignty has not been compromised; and the reserve backing allows the central bank to earn revenue by investing such assets in foreign countries. This covers the expense of the currency issue and the bank's upkeep costs, and may provide financial aid to problem banks and dividends to the state budget. It should be stressed that a currency board needs sound and liberal monetary policy support, an open economy, and free international financial and trade relations. At the end of 1997 the foreign loan liability of Estonia's central government and municipalities was only 7 percent of GDP, and overall surplus of the Estonian consolidated budget was 2.4 percent of GDP. On the other hand, it is possible that after some time the real exchange rate may become overvalued and force devaluation, undermine monetary confidence, and cause the economy to become uncompetitive (Dale 1997, p. 35).

There are always people who complain that the foreign exchange rate is the reason for economic failure. The most dangerous sentiment to a currency board system is one that casts doubt on its security. Steps in the direction of devaluation or abandonment of the currency board are likely to bring about inflation, given the arguments for covert efforts designed for cutting costs and improving the country's competitiveness on the part of some policy makers. In 1994 the Bank of Estonia introduced forward contracts at the official exchange rate (8 EEK = 1 DM) with a duration up to 7 years, in order to dispel doubts about the continued existence of the currency board. By December 1994, the total amount of these contracts was worth 1,428 million kroons (DM 178.5 million), which formed about 18 percent of the kroon's cover by the Bank of Estonia.

The authors are of the opinion that a currency board by itself acts as a good check on inflation. If there are substantial amounts of foreign money in circulation, fixed exchange rates provide an even more effective nominal anchor (Calvo and Végh 1993, p. 36). Sound monetary policy raises the possibility of borrowing the necessary resources to start a currency board. The later profit from the currency board system will allow payback of the loans with big returns.

Implementation of the currency board arrangement and fixing the Estonian kroon to the German mark has been a solid nominal anchor to the economic recovery and development of the economy. Of course, the fixed exchange rate regime was only one (but maybe the most important) component of the Estonian economic policy framework for macroeconomic stabilization. We must mention also other policies, such as the liberal external trade regime, or tight fiscal discipline, which have been also important factors of the macroeconomic stabilization. Main indicators characterizing Estonian economic development during 1995–98 are presented in Table 6.12.

Economic growth in Estonia has been moderate. In 1997, real GDP of Estonia formed 77.9 percent of the 1989 level (see Table 1.1). Although this economic recovery indicator is less than in the Central European countries (average 92.1 percent), this is one of the highest in the former Soviet Union (CIS average 56.1 percent), and it is also highest in comparison with other Baltic states. As we can see from Table 6.12, moderate GDP growth continued in 1998, in spite of the negative impact of external factors (in particular, the Russian crises).

Finally, we would like to recommend that those with doubts about the stability and duration of fixed exchange rates examine the Austrian experience. For the past two decades, Austria's monetary policy has been successfully geared to keeping the schilling's nominal exchange rate stable vis-à-vis other "hard" European currencies, by pegging it to an anti-

Table 6.12
Main Indicators of the Estonian Economic Development, 1995–98

	1995	1996	1997	1998
Nominal GDP (in billion kroons)	41.3	52.4	65.1	73.2
Real GDP growth (%)	4.3	4.0	11.4	4.0
Consumer price index (%)	29.0	23.1	11.2	8.2
Growth of real wages (%)	6.2	2.1	7.6	6.3
Real effective exchange rate of the Estonian kroon, REER (%, CPI based)	18.0	9.7	3.3	12.6
Current account deficit (% of GDP)	−4.6	−9.6	−12.9	−9.0
Exports (% of GDP)	71.3	67.2	77.2	78.3
Imports (% of GDP)	79.3	78.7	88.6	87.1
Government deficit/surplus (% of GDP)	−1.2	−1.5	2.1	−0.2
Total assets of commercial banks (in billion kroons)	15.5	22.9	40.6	41.0
Banks' loan portfolio (in billion kroons)	10.3	14.4	19.5	22.5
Capitalization of securities market (in billion kroons)	3.2	13.4	24.5	15.1
Short-term loan rates (%, end of the year)	16.0	13.7	19.8	16.7
Long-term loan rates (%, end of the year)	15.8	13.9	11.2	16.3
Time deposit rates (%, end of the year)	7.2	5.3	12.2	8.1

Source: Bank of Estonia.

inflationary currency, the mark (see Austrian Exchange Rate Policy 1995).

THE FUTURE PERSPECTIVES OF THE ESTONIAN CURRENCY BOARD ARRANGEMENT

The main aim of Estonian macroeconomic policy is to continue preparations for integration with the EU. As it is argued, from a strictly monetary policy point of view, Estonia has been a de facto member of the euro zone already for six years (Ross 1999). Estonia adopted a nominal external anchor for introducing the currency board arrangement and fixing the exchange rate of the domestic currency to the German mark during the monetary reform in 1992. And so, Estonia was already connected with the European monetary policy.

Although there were also other options (for example, to peg the Estonian kroon to the euro with relatively wide fluctuation bands—see Pautola and Backe 1998, p. 98), since January 1, 1999, the Estonian kroon is fixed strictly also to the euro, both de facto and de jure. Decree No. 39 from December 31, 1998, by the president of the Bank of Estonia stipulated that the exchange rate of the Estonian kroon is fixed to the euro at EUR 1 = EEK 15.6466, which is equivalent to fixing the kroon to the German mark at DM 1 = EEK 8.

In its statement, the board of the Bank of Estonia declared: "Eesti Pank assures that the introduction of the euro by the 11 Member States on 1 January 1999 will not cause any changes in Estonian monetary policy. Estonia will not deviate from its monetary policy based on currency board arrangement and fixed exchange rate. That means that the exchange rate of Estonian kroon against the German mark will remain on the present level, i.e. 8 to 1. However, it also means that starting from already 1 January 1999 the Estonian kroon will be fixed against the euro" (Eesti Pank 1998). The Bank of Estonia also announced that, relating to the introduction of the single currency, certain formal and technical changes in the operational framework of the Estonian monetary policy will be made.

The question is, What are the future perspectives of the currency board arrangement in Estonia? Or, will the currency board arrangement constitute a viable monetary framework in the long-run perspective? As it is pointed out, for example, by Pautola and Backe, there are two main subsets of issues in order to answer these questions (Pautola and Backe 1998, pp. 93–101): (1) whether the balance of economic advantages and drawbacks of the currency board arrangement changed over time, and how it will change in the future; (2) what relevance the prospects of the EU integration have and will have for Estonia with its currency board—that is, will a currency board arrangement be a suitable monetary framework for joining the EU?

The first step toward the EU for Estonia (as for other associated member countries of Central and Eastern Europe) is to meet needed economic, social, and legal requirements for EU membership. Although Estonian authorities declared already in 1997 that the currency board will provide a good starting point for Estonia's integration into the EU and into the European Monetary Union (see Eesti Pank 1997), we must look at the possibilities of fulfilling the Maastricht convergence criteria in the conditions of operating the currency board.

The Maastricht convergence criteria state that to qualify for the European Monetary Union, which started on January 1, 1999, the following criteria will have to have been met:

1. the rate of inflation cannot be more than 1.5 percentage points above the average of the three best-performing member states;
2. long-term interest rates cannot be more than 2 percentage points above the same benchmark;
3. the budget deficit cannot exceed 3 percent of GDP, unless this ratio has declined "substantially and continuously," or the excess over the reference value is "exceptional and temporary";
4. public debt cannot exceed 60 percent of GDP, unless the ratio is diminishing "sufficiently" and approaching the reference value at a "satisfactory pace";
5. the exchange rate should have observed the "normal margins" of the Exchange Rate Mechanism (ERM) of the European Monetary System (EMS) for the two preceding years.

It is clear that Estonia has no serious problems with the fiscal criteria: both public debt and fiscal deficit are below the stipulated criteria, mainly due to the currency board arrangement. Also the pegged exchange rate regime on the basis of the currency board arrangement is suitable to participate in a fixed exchange rate regime centered around the euro. As it has been pointed out (see, for example, Berengaut et al. 1998, p. 75), more efforts will be needed regarding the other two financial criteria, inflation and interest rates.

The inflation rate in Estonia (as in other EU candidate countries) is still significantly above the EU average, and especially above the rates of inflation of the best-performing states. It seems, that even more problematic is the issue of long-term interest rates. In reality, Estonia, with highly underdeveloped long-term capital markets, is still in transition to well-developed market economies, and the development of financial markets will be an important prerequisite for meeting the criterion on long-term interest rate stability. We may agree with the opinion that the absence of well-developed financial markets in Estonia is an important sign of the unreadiness for participation in the European Monetary Union.

In general, there is a clear trend toward greater exchange rate flexibility for developing and transition countries during the past several years. According to the IMF survey (1997), there has been a marked shift away from single-currency pegs since the early 1980s: in 1975, 87 percent of developing countries had some type of pegged exchange rate and only 10 percent had flexible rates; by 1985, these proportions were respectively 71 percent and 25 percent; by 1996, the proportions were 45 percent and 52 percent.

Experience has shown that exiting from a pegged exchange rate regime has often been involuntary, as a result of speculative attacks. Countries that have exited from pegged-rate arrangements have generally waited until their domestic currency was under pressure. The main characteristics of such a situation are that reserves declined, output and export growth slowed, and expansionary monetary policy led to high inflation, overvaluation of the domestic currency, and large external imbalances due to policies that encourage imports and limit exports. In addition, speculative crises are associated with high unemployment, weak banking systems, and high ratios of public debt. There is a lot of literature about the experience of exits from pegged exchange rate regimes—more recently, about Chile, Israel, Mexico, Poland, and Thailand (see Eichengreen et al. 1998).

During 1997–98, there were some signs of financial crises and speculative attacks against the Estonian kroon due both to the developments in global markets (first of all, Asian crises and Russian crises) and developments in domestic markets (the bursting of the 1997 stock exchange bubble, overoptimistic and risky attitudes toward the opportunities of the Eastern European markets, increased current account deficit, etc.). Some authors mentioned that spillover effects from the Asian crises have been felt in financial and foreign exchange most clearly in Russia, Ukraine, and Estonia (see Valdivieso 1998, p. 13). This is true in this sense that in Estonia we can mention a remarkable degree of international integration of domestic financial markets. As a result, there were in Estonia both external and domestic pressures in financial markets, which were associated with a large current account deficit and a steep rise in equity prices (stock exchange bubble).

Fortunately, policy makers learned lessons from this financial crisis experience. The main aims of the economic policy (as a result of the financial crisis) were formulated by the adviser to the Bank of Estonia, Raimund Hagelberg (see Hagelberg 1998, pp. 12–13):

1. maintain the stability of the monetary system, taking advantage of the existing possibilities of the currency board arrangement;
2. increase trust in the banking system (and the entire financial system) by improving legislation, strengthening banking super-

vision, making the operation of the law enforcement and the legal system more efficient, and proceeding from good banking practice;

3. guarantee the balance of the state budget and state funds proceeding from real income and the most essential expenditures;
4. continue allocations to the stabilization reserve and adopt legislation that would allow its use only in the case of real emergencies;
5. start acting more savingly in both personal and public consumption, which must be accompanied by the stability of the Estonian domestic currency and growing credibility of the banking system and other financial institutions;
6. reconsider the current investment policy, proceeding from the interests of increasing Estonia's competitiveness and export potential.

In general, implementation of these main economic policy objectives has been successful. At the moment, we do not see any urgent reason to abandon the currency board arrangement in Estonia. We agree with the statement that "one may conclude that the Estonian currency board can be maintained if fiscal policy, including the envisaged further tightening, is implemented as planned, if it succeeds in curbing the current account deficit, and if limited monetary measures are sufficient to keep bank lending under control and to address potential complications resulting from capital flow volatility" (Pautola and Backe 1988, pp. 97–98).

Even in the long-run perspective, it may become unnecessary to abandon the currency board arrangement. Main problems are connected with the high current account deficit; further widening could cause serious pressures to devalue the Estonian kroon and abandon the currency board. Another important negative factor is that domestic credit expansion in real terms has been rapid during the past several years, funded by massive borrowing from abroad due to the sizable interest rate differential. Doubt about the soundness of the banking sector is also mentioned among the greatest threats to the credibility of a currency board arrangement (Enoch and Gulde 1997).

Problems mentioned are not serious. Recent developments in the Estonian balance of payments are presented in Table 6.13. The slowdown of the foreign capital inflow (Table 6.14) and the decline in domestic demand caused remarkable reduction of the current account deficit during

Table 6.13
Estonian Balance of Payments, 1996–98 (in million kroons)

	1996	1997	1998 Q1	1998 Q2	1998 Q3	1998 Q4	1998 Total
Current Account	−4807	−7813	−2077	−1710	−1504	−1041	−6332
Trade and services	−6043	−7423	−2213	−1680	−1699	−1478	−7070
Trade balance	−12288	−15655	−3615	−4509	−4452	−3148	−15724
Services: net	6245	8232	1402	2829	2753	1670	8654
Income: net	26	−2011	−325	−577	−297	−143	−1342
Transfers: net	1210	1620	462	547	492	580	2081
Capital and Financial Account	6396	10953	1040	3473	371	1894	6778
Capital account	−8	−2	10	4	9	2	25
Financial account	6404	10955	1030	3469	362	1892	6753
Direct investments	1330	1781	1218	872	3237	2544	7871
Portfolio investments	1784	3655	992	1322	−1285	−1008	22
Other investments	3290	5519	−1181	1275	−1590	356	−1140
Errors and omissions	−361	−369	−97	269	−127	−364	−319
Overall balance	1228	2771	−1134	2032	−1260	488	126

Source: Bank of Estonia.

1998 (see also Eesti Pank 1999). In 1998, the current account deficit was 10 percent smaller than in 1997, which points to the improvement of the external balance of the Estonian economy. Since the monetary reforms until 1997, the net inflow of capital had exceeded the growth of demand for imports, which resulted in the growth of foreign currency reserves and the surplus of the overall balance of payments. In 1998 the increase of the foreign currency reserves stopped and the overall balance of payments had no surplus.

In 1998, the openness of the Estonian economy increased—foreign trade turnover of goods and services amounted to 168 percent of the GDP (166 percent in 1997), which is one of the highest in the world. The biggest share of the current account deficit still derived from the foreign trade balance, although the foreign trade balance deficit ratio to the GDP fell from 24 percent in 1997 to 21 percent in 1998. The growth rate of exports continued to outstrip that of imports and was 5.9 per-

Table 6.14
Inflows of Foreign Direct Investment in the Transition Economies, 1995–97 (in millions U.S. $)

	1995	1996	1997	January–June 1998	Per capita, 1997	FDI/GDP %, 1997
Eastern Europe	9159	7577	9100	5100	82	2.7
Albania	70	90	48	24	14	2.1
Bulgaria	90	190	489	108	58	4.8
Croatia	88	533	388	494	86	2.0
Czech Republic	2562	1428	1300	589	127	2.5
Hungary	4453	1983	2085	951	209	4.7
Poland	1134	2768	3077	2093	80	2.3
Romania	419	263	1215	544	54	3.5
Slovakia	157	206	161	240	30	0.8
Slovenia	176	185	321	34	167	1.8
Macedonia	9	11	16	22	7	0.5
Baltic States	457	684	1142	514	149	5.8
Estonia	205	150	267	144	183	5.7
Latvia	180	382	521	165	211	9.4
Lithuania	73	152	355	205	95	3.7
European CIS	2362	3097	7116	1681	33	1.4
Belarus	15	73	192	55	19	1.5
Moldova	64	24	60	38	14	3.2
Russia	2016	2479	6241	1161	42	1.3
Ukraine	267	521	623	427	12	1.3
Total	11978	11358	17358	7295	52	2.0

Source: United Nations 1988, pp. 123–24, 177.

centage points higher. The share of the EU in Estonia's foreign trade amounted to about 70 percent (Eesti Pank 1999).

The structure of the financial account also improved in 1998. The short-term loan capital was replaced by direct investment capital, and the flows of more volatile portfolio investment capital were in balance. The flow of foreign direct investments increased in 1998. It was 7.8 billion Estonian kroons, that is, about 4.5 times larger than in 1997 (Table 6.13). It is notable that the main source of direct investment in Estonia was the strategic investors attracted to the banking sector (49 percent). Investments in the industry sector made up only 20 percent of the total volume of foreign direct investments. The bulk of the foreign capital came from Finland and Sweden (Eesti Pank 1999).

Changes took place in the Estonian banking sector in 1998. Growth of banks' loan portfolios was lower than in 1995–97 (see Table 6.12), and the liquidity position of commercial banks improved. The Bank of Estonia adopted several radical measures to prevent possible instability in the Estonian banking sector. Some banks were merged, and in some banks bankruptcy procedures were initiated. As a result of such consolidation process, the number of commercial banks in the Estonian banking market fell to six (in 1992, there were forty-two banks operating in Estonia).

Problems in the banking sector were first and foremost due to erroneous financial and management decisions made in the changed and tightening competition environment. The changed economic environment had a significant effect on the Estonian banking sector, including negative effects from the Russian crises, particularly on smaller banks. The largest Estonian banks merged: the Estonian Savings Bank (market share 21 percent) merged with Hansapank (market share 24 percent), and the Bank of Tallinn (market share 7 percent) merged with the Union Bank of Estonia (market share 26 percent). As a result, the interest of Scandinavian banks against Estonian banks rose: Swedish *Swedbank* acquired 59 percent of the Hansapank and *Skandinaviska Enskilda Banken* acquired 32 percent of the Union Bank of Estonia.

Of course, the Estonian kroon is not a miracle currency and the currency board arrangement is not the only possible choice for the Estonian economic policy. Nevertheless, taking into account recent developments in the Estonian economy and the credibility of government and monetary authorities announcements, the authors of this chapter do not see serious reasons for abandonment of the fixed exchange rate in the framework of the currency board arrangement.

CONCLUSION

At the time of the writing of this chapter, nearly seven years had elapsed since the Estonian currency reform. The Estonian economy had reached the upturn stage, the balance of payments showed a modest surplus, Estonia's external debt was minimal, the inflation rate was declining, the unemployment rate was comparatively low, and real income was growing. It seems reasonable to conclude that this success is positively related to the country's currency board system, supported by liberal monetary and economic policy.

After the national independence in 1991, it was natural for Estonia to choose a currency board system. The economic stability, resources, and experience necessary to introduce a flexible exchange rate regime did not exist at the time. Instead, a monetary system that met the actual economic and financial situation in Estonia, suitable to its banking and management skills, was opted for. The currency board endowed the Estonian kroon with confidence, which helped attract foreign capital to support the country's reforms and supply the resources necessary to back its currency. Another key to the success of the currency board is the extremely liberal monetary policy applied. This created a favorable environment for developing the financial infrastructure necessary for the progress of reform, and the rapid integration of Estonia's monetary system and economy with the international economy.

There are no serious arguments that would compel Estonia to give up the currency board system and its liberal monetary policy. On the contrary, these principles amount to an important mechanism which allows Estonia's economy to develop consistently, and to retain and improve its competitiveness in the world market. A small country has no better road to social welfare. This view is shared by the board of the Bank of Estonia and the government and opposition in the parliament. Recent macroeconomic developments and introduced economic policy measures affirm this general conclusion.

REFERENCES

Austrian Exchange Rate Policy and European Monetary Integration. *Selected Issues*. E. E. Hochreiter, ed. Oesterreichische Nationalbank working paper, no. 19, p. 71, 1995.

Balino, T. J. T., and C. Enoch. IMF Staff. *Currency Board Arrangements: Issues and Experiences*. IMF occasional paper, no. 151. Washington, D.C.: IMF, 1997.

Berengaut, J., et al. *The Baltic Countries: From Economic Stabilization to EU Accession*. IMF occasional paper, no. 173. Washington, D.C.: IMF, 1998.

Calvo, G. A., and C. A. Végh. "Currency Substitution in High Inflation Countries." *Finance & Development*, March 1993, pp. 34–37.

Camard, W. *Lessons from the Currency Board Arrangement in Lithua-*

nia. IMF paper on policy analysis and assessment, no. 96/1. Washington, D.C.: IMF, 1996.

Currency Board Arrangement More Widely Used. IMF Survey 1997, February 24, pp. 54–57.

Dale, R. *Currency Boards. Review of Economics in Transition.* Helsinki: Bank of Finland, 1997, no. 3, pp. 23–36.

Dillon, P., and V. Vensel. *The Estonian Currency Board: A Case for Fiscal Discipline and Monetary Bondage.* Claremont policy briefs, no. 96–02.

Eesti Pank. The 1997–1998 Programme for the Economic Policy of the Government of Estonia and Eesti Pank. Press release, November 11, 1999. Http://www.ee/epbe.

———. Statement of the Board of Eesti Pank Regarding the Launch of the European Economic and Monetary Union Third Stage and the Introduction of the Euro. Statement, December 10, 1998. Http://www.ee/epbe.

———. Comments on the 1998 Preliminary Balance of Payments of Estonia. *Eesti Pank Newsletter*, no. 1 (200), March 20, 1999. Http://www.ee/epbe

Eichengreen, B., P. Masson, et al. *Exit Strategies: Policy Options for Countries Seeking Greater Exchange Rate Flexibility.* IMF occasional paper, no. 168, Washington, D.C.: IMF, 1998.

Enoch, C., and A. M. Gulde. *Making a Currency Board Operational.* IMF paper on policy analysis and assessment, no. 97/10. Washington, D.C.: IMF, 1997.

Fischer, S. "Maintaining Price Stability." *Finance & Development*, December 1996, pp. 34–37.

Ghatak, S. *Monetary Economics in Developing Countries.* 2nd ed. St. Martin's Press, 1995, p. 226.

Ghosh, A. A., A.-M. Gulde, J. D. Ostry, and H. Wolf. *Does the Exchange Rate Regime Matter for Inflation and Growth.* IMF Economic Issues, no. 2, September 1996, p. 13.

Ghosh, A. R. et al. *Currency Boards—The Ultimate Fix?* IMF working paper, no. 98/8. Washington, D.C.: IMF, January 1998.

Hagelberg, R. "Some Observations that Might Help to Understand More Accurately the Developments in the Estonian Economic Environment." *Eesti Pank Bulletin*, no. 6 (41), 1998, pp. 9–13.

Hanke, S. H., L. Jonung, and K. Schuler. "Estonia: It's not a Currency Board System." *Transition* 1993, no. 1, p. 12.

International Monetary Fund. *World Economic Outlook, October 1997:*

A Survey by the Staff of the International Monetary Fund. World Economic and Financial Surveys. Washington, D.C.: IMF, 1997.

Isachsen, A. J., C. B. Hamilton, and T. Gulfason. *Basic Economics: From Plan Market to Market.* Stragest Ltd., Tallinn, 1994, p. 372.

Kalda, T. George Soros: "Establishing a Stable and Convertible Currency is the Basis for Estonia's Success." *Estonian Kroon*, no. 4, 1994, July, pp. 24–25.

Kallas, S., and M. Sörg. *Currency Reform Transforming the Estonian Economy.* Ed. O. Lugus and G. A. Hachey, Jr. International Center for Economic Growth, Tallinn, 1995, pp. 71–91.

Laar, M. "Estonian Policy—Priorities and Perspectives." Address at a Colloquy of the German Foreign Policy Association, Bonn, June 28, 1993, p. 5.

Lainela, S., and P. Sutela. *The Baltic Economies in Transition.* Helsinki: Bank of Finland, 1994, p. 138.

Langmore, J. "Restructuring Economic and Financial Power. The Potential Role of a Foreign Exchange—Transaction Levy." *Futures*, March 1995, vol. 27, no. 2, pp. 189–94.

Pautola, N., and P. Backe. "Currency Boards in Central and Eastern Europe: Past Experience and Future Perspectives." *Focus on Transition*, Oesterreichische Nationalbank, April 1998, pp. 72–113.

Ross, M. *Estonian Monetary System and Euro.* A paper for "EURO" no. 47, II/1999. Http://www.epbe.ee/kppo.

Sahay, R., and C. Végh. "Dollarization in Transition Economies." *Finance & Development*, March 1995, pp. 36–39.

Sörg, M. "Estonian Strategies in the Reconstruction of Its Monetary System." In *The Competitiveness of Financial Institutions and Centres in Europe.* Ed. D. E. Fair and R. J. Raymond. Kluwer Academic Publishers, 1994, pp. 171–82.

———. "Estonia Currency Board and Economic Performance." *South African Journal of Economic and Management Sciences*, 1 (3), September 1998, pp. 463–82.

Valdivieso, L. M. *Macroeconomic Developments in the Baltics, Russia, and Other Countries of the Former Soviet Union, 1992–97.* IMF occasional paper, no. 175. Washington, D.C.: IMF, 1998.

United Nations. *Economic Survey of Europe, 1998*, no. 3. New York and Geneva: United Nations, 1998.

7

The Currency Board in Bulgaria: Is It a Solution or the Economic Consequences of Failed Reforms?

Iliana Zloch-Christy

The currency board was introduced in Bulgaria in July 1997. It was suggested by the IMF as an alternative means of addressing economic policy dilemmas in the country. (Bulgaria experienced hyperinflation in the fall of 1996 and early 1997.)

After reading the Bulgarian press and professional journals, I have the impression that Bulgarian politicians, government officials, and scholars even more than two years after its introduction still do not realize the importance of this institution and the political, economic, and social consequences in the short and medium terms.

This chapter attempts to answer the question whether the proposed and accepted currency board arrangement is a solution to the economic problems of this country. The structure is as follows: after the introductory remarks, the first part presents an overview of the hyperinflation and stabilization in some countries in the past. The second part poses the question of why a currency board and what the alternatives are. The third part attempts to answer whether it is a solution. The concluding remarks summarize the findings of the chapter.

Former World Bank chief economist Michael Bruno in a book published in 1993 (p. 14, footnote 17) cites a statement by a colleague of his during his term as a governor of the Bank of Israel in the hyperinflationary period in Israel in the 1980s: “Has the situation deteriorated badly enough to be good for us policy advisors?” Following the statement of Bruno the question arises: If the situation deteriorated so badly in Bulgaria in 1996, was it good for the policy advisers, and if yes, was the currency board a solution, good enough for the country? But before answering this question, let me present a brief overview of the hyperinflation in other countries and their policy responses.

Inflation and hyperinflation are twentieth-century phenomena associated with printing paper money. The classical cases of hyperinflation are the German, Polish, Austrian, and Hungarian, as well as the post–World War II inflations in Europe. The four countries that had the biggest price increase in the 1950–85 period were the three Latin American countries Argentina, Bolivia, and Brazil, and Israel in the Middle East. Other countries with hyperinflationary crises were Chile (1975), Mexico (1988), and the two European countries Yugoslavia (1990) and Poland (1990). Latin America holds the record of hyperinflation after World War II (Bruno 1993, p. 18).

Hyperinflation is associated with a monthly rate of price increase exceeding 50 percent. It is a serious macroeconomic problem and usually takes place as the result of an internal economic and political crisis associated with a failed or inadequate response to external shocks and big domestic and external debt. All inflationary cases have common roots—internal imbalances and large budget deficits. The nature of the inflationary process as well as the policy adjustments have varied across countries, but the economic, political, and social seriousness of tackling this macroeconomic problem associated with low or negative growth is the same for all of them. Extremely high inflation rates make it virtually impossible for firms and households to have a clear picture of the present, and obviously of the future structure of relative prices with all the disastrous consequences for drop in production, decreased investment activity, depletion of ressources, and destruction of human capital. All that leaves a vacuum that may take years, even decades, to fill.[1]

In all of the countries the hyperinflationary periods appear to have been intense and explosive processes with high (more than three-digit) annual inflation lasting no more than twenty months (Bruno 1993, p. 20). In all of the countries the end of the hyperinflationary process took place once the government signaled a credible shift of policy and instituted sharp reforms such as a credible fiscal balance and a strong central bank. All that led to quick and dramatic change in private-sector expectations and inflationary behavior, which put an end to the inflationary spiral. In these cases of hyperinflation, the possibility of using a currency board was not discussed. As was discussed in Chapters 3 to 6, after World War I currency boards existed in a number of colonies, effectively placing them on the gold standard. And as is well known the reintroduction of the gold standard in the developed West (United Kingdom, France, United States) and in many other countries in that period caused recession in almost all of them.

As discussed in Chapter 3, the currency board is a financial institution replacing the existence of a central bank (abolished or transformed) and is associated with a strictly monetary discipline where no more domestic money can be printed and put in circulation at a fixed exchange rate than the existing foreign exchange reserves. As Stanley Fischer briefly defines it, "the monetary theory of the currency board is exactly that of the gold standard" and it "provides one example of a truly fixed rate regime, with the strongest of commitments to the exchange rate peg" (1996, p. 37).

The currency board was introduced in the 1990s, for example, in Argentina (1991), Estonia (1992), and Lithuania (1994), with the intention not to end a monetary crisis, but to avoid such crises in the future. In the case of Argentina it was introduced after a painful period of protracted inflation and hyperinflation during the 1980s.

WHY A CURRENCY BOARD?

The currency board is associated with policies aimed at achieving macroeconomic stabilization and in the case of the present developments in Bulgaria with handling inflationary recession. It is introduced when other possible approaches, such as price, wage, and money supply controls, are seen as not credible. It is a harsh institutional arrangement to stabilize the national currency since the government has no room for flexibility if policy adjustments are needed.

As alternatives to the currency board two policy approaches dominate stabilization efforts: first, a stable peg policy (fixed exchange rate) associated with considerable foreign exchange reserves, and second, a floating exchange rate associated mainly with high domestic interest rates. These policies, of course, are monitored and directed by the central bank. And again, we turn to a statement by Stanley Fischer in an article where he points to the importance of central bank independence: "I advocate central bank independence" (1996, p. 37). He also stresses that countries with adjustable pegs have had lower inflation on average during 1979–93.

The question arises: Why a currency board given the other two policy alternatives? The general answer is: it depends on the credibility of the government and its policies. Since the currency board was introduced voluntarily only in a few cases, this fact suggests the short answer: it depends if the government is seen by international creditors as credible or not. All that summarizes the main reasons for the currency board: lack of credibility of government policies plus lack of foreign exchange reserves and access to international capital markets.

What was the policy of Bulgaria in combating the inflationary recession in recent years when the country de facto was run by socialist (old communist) governments? The short answer is obvious: unsuccessful. The longer answer is that given the serious macroeconomic imbalances in Bulgaria, its governments have been tempted to increase the money supply, which enables them to increase government spending without having to rely on the highly inefficient tax-collecting system with the limited possibilities of borrowing from the public and budgetary problems on the revenue side.

As stated in my 1996 edited book, *Bulgaria in a Time of Change: Economic and Political Dimensions* (pp. 154–56), eliminating inflation proved to be too ambitious a goal for all of the governments after 1989 given the economic collapse of the country. The ineffective monetary policies proved difficult to sustain because of populist social and political considerations which led to the vicious cycle of inflation and higher unemployment. Bulgarian policy makers learned little from the experience of a number of developing countries and the basic lessons that a failure to adjust to the constraints imposed by the balance of payments, huge external debt, and growing domestic debt in a situation of reduced internal productive capacity will lead to (hyper)inflation and disaster.

It is obvious that Bulgarian policy makers do not understand the development of crises and have little (or no) ability to avert them. They were not able to tackle the problem of living with inflation over time, focusing more on structural reforms (institutional reforms, demonopolization, privatization). This is, of course, a risky approach and requires great sophistication of economic policy and abilities of the policy makers, obviously too difficult a task for the present Bulgarian elites.

It might be interesting to mention here that one of the former finance ministers of Brazil said some years ago: "If inflation is a horse, I know how to ride it." The Bulgarian economic policy makers did not know how to tackle this challenge (and of course did not comprehend the issue of profit inflation) and did not make any effort to work on a long-term vision of reform steps encompassing areas such as institution building, stabilization, privatization, industrial policy, and foreign investments, (among others). In 1997–99 they were confronted with the need to introduce the currency board since they were not able to negotiate any other policy approach with the international creditors of the country. The caretaker government of the so-called democratic opposition signed an agreement with the IMF for a currency board in 1997. Even though the victory of the democratic opposition at the elections in April 1997 was expected, the international institutions insisted on the introduction of the currency board. And this fact speaks for itself.

WAS A CURRENCY BOARD A SOLUTION?

The discussion in the previous section shows that Bulgarian economic policy makers are obviously at a crossroad. Some of them see the currency board as a kind of panacea for the troubled Bulgarian economy. Former adviser to the socialist (former communist) governments I. Angelov states that the introduction of the currency board "is the only possibility to stop the economic collapse" (*Sega*, no. 4, January 30–February 5, 1997, pp. 30–32, p. 30). Was it really?

My answer is: I doubt it. In the following discussion I briefly explain why. The currency board is in principle an exchange rate approach to combating inflation. It presupposes something that is rarely given: there must be absolutely no difference between the domestic rate of price increase and that of the country (or countries) whose currency (or basket of currencies) serve(s) as the key currency/currencies. In May 1997 it was announced that the mark would serve as an anchor currency and this arrangement was made as of July 1, 1997. Since January 1, 1999 the anchor currency is the euro. If there is a price increase differential—and in the Bulgarian case this is unavoidable given the collapse of the economy—the consequence is something that might be called a *repressed depreciation*, since the exchange rate is fixed. The consequences are numerous, but I should point out here as in Chapter 3 the following four:

1. The Bulgarian lev appreciates in real terms with a negative impact on the country's export and competitiveness.

2. The trade balance and the current account deteriorate.
3. Balance-of-payments financing is urgently needed, thus causing the external balance to deteriorate further.
4. Real incomes decline, given the downward pressure on the value of the currency.

Currency board arrangements might put severe strains on the banking system, as Stanley Fischer stresses (1996, p. 37), since there is no lender of last resort (central bank). This does not apply if the country has built up a large excess of cover for the domestic monetary base (like in Hong Kong, where the currency board has functioned for many years). This obviously is not the case in Bulgaria. It might be interesting to cite here again Fischer's statement that the currency board can "work well if fiscal policy is highly responsible and the commercial banks are international" (p. 37). An intriguing question arises: How many international commercial banks have licenses in Bulgaria and from which countries are they? Given the low international rating, Bulgarian banks have restricted access to the international capital markets. And these are major dilemmas for the economic policy makers in this country, in a situation of giving up on central banking. And one more remark in this regard: as was stressed earlier in this chapter, in principle, a currency board arrangement is giving up on central banking, and is based on gold standard monetary policy rules. As its well-known advocate, Steve Hanke, has put it, "it represents a historic deviation from IMF orthodoxy" (*Transition*, vol. 8, no.1, February 1997, p. 8). He stresses further that the IMF has asserted in its programs that central banks are lenders of last resort and that the provision of credits are engines for economic development.

It is hard to believe that Bulgarian economic policy makers and politicians look at the present currency board arrangement as a *consensus of stagnation*. And in this regard it would be interesting to try to approach the question of what comprises *economic success*, which hardly can be heard in a discussion in the Bulgarian public life. Bulgarian politicians often point out that in the 1997–99 period there has been political stability in the country, overlooking the point that in less developed countries, like Bulgaria, such stability is often the result of social and economic depression. But let us turn back to the issue of *economic success*. What is economic success? For example, is currency stabilization a success and is it sustainable? The answer is not clear. One of the lessons learned in the past several years is that it is nonsense to believe that if you unify exchange rates, eliminate import restrictions, or introduce a currency board, you are on the right track. But is it all so simple? Are these the only conditions required to stabilize the economy? The answer is "no." They are not sufficient conditions. Experience in many developing countries shows that such economic policy is critically important and particularly dangerous in those cases in which domestic economies lack a long-term development program, relevant state administrative capacities, and a solid institutional base. All that was discussed at length by G. Kolodko in Chapter 1. In addition, I should also mention here that the present situation in Bulgaria resembles one that might be called *democlatura*, given the strong presence in the political and business life of the former communist nomenclatura, the state control of the media (among others), and the still prevailing communist mentality in social interactions.

All this indicates that it will be only a question of time until voices for abolishing the currency board will be heard. Since it is obviously a classical deflationary arrangement with a drop in production and investment and a rise in unemployment, the pressure from the trade unions for its abolition will increase. Many losing enterprises and small businesses will be forced to restructure or close, and banks that provided loans to such enterprises will be bankrupted. Decline of output and rise of unemployment are logical consequences. Ironically I do agree here with the statement of Steve Hanke that the currency board "will satisfy two necessary, though not sufficient conditions . . . to reform: stable money and monetary stability" (p. 9). These conditions are not sufficient to reform because stabilization is only one step of the reform effort. And "resurging" the gold standard is an obsolete intellectual tool to be applied to the troubled Bulgarian economy. There is a danger of underestimating the fact that limited knowledge on the part of the Bulgarian economic policy makers, elected leaders, and voters has been an important source of monetary policy mistakes. The failures in monetary policy arise not just from dynamic inconsistency, but more important from imperfect understanding of the economy and the effects of policy.

Social unrest is a probable scenario, given the social chaos and rising criminality. Remember the January 1997 mass demonstrations against the socialist government. The question arises as to who will lead the new demonstrations in the future and against whom. These are obviously not only questions of economic policy but serious questions that require strategic long-term thinking on the part of the economic and political elites in Bulgaria. There is an urgent need to create teams of professional economists to work on the strategy (and alternative strategies) of economic policy reform in the country.

All this indicates that the currency board should be seen not only as a *political* decision of the moment, but as a serious institutional arrangement which might do more harm than good to the country for many years, even decades. It is an illusion to think that stabilizing unstable inflationary expectations, which, of course, can be achieved rapidly with a currency board, solves the main problem—eliminating stable inflationary expectations altogether.[2] There is a danger that a currency board itself might become increasingly a factor of uncertainty, thus contributing to further destabilization of the economy. With liquidity in shorter supply, delays in privatization, almost no banking restructuring, restrictions on central bank lending to the government and the banks, and low flows of foreign investments, barter transactions[3] will play an important role, the net result being a massive loss of efficiency, destruction of human capital, and rise of transaction costs. It might take many years to repair the damage caused by the means that were used to combat inflation. All this indicates that it is an illusion to expect a rise in economic growth after the initial stabilization when the currency board is introduced. And what matters for the future is the rise of economic growth, productivity, and living standards. This should be the goal of macroeconomic stabilization: to create the grounds for economic growth and employment.[4] It should be also mentioned here, that as discussed by Pautola in Chapter 4, the currency board raises questions for the future integration and EU membership. Just to mention one of them: a currency board country cannot fully participate in the institutionalized exchange rate cooperation of a standard EU type, which requires flexible use of interest rates. And this further indicates the need to reassess the currency board in Bulgaria.

CONCLUSION

By combating inflation there are different mechanisms for achieving price stability. The currency board is the harshest and is obviously not the most efficient since its deflationary effects are strong. Politics is the art of the possible. Economic policy is the art of choosing the best strategy for the country. I doubt if the Bulgarian policy makers realize this challenge. To conclude briefly: the problem of Bulgaria is not its currency but its government. These are the economic consequences of the last Bulgarian governments (with their cleptonomics) as well as of the deeply rooted communist culture in the Bulgarian society. Bulgaria continues to live in the realm of the impossible.

NOTES

1. It might be interesting to mention here the statement of J. M. Keynes for the danger and destructionary forces of inflation: "Lenin was certainly right. There is no subtler, no surer means of overturning the existing basis of society than to debauch the currency. The process engages all the hidden forces of economic law on the side of destruction, and does it in a manner which no one man in a million is able to diagnose" (1988, p. 236).

2. According to official publications the main macroeconomic indicators deteriorated in 1997: real GDP − 8 percent (over the previous year), gross industrial production − 11.5 percent, consumer price inflation 578.5 percent, unemployment rate 13.5 percent (compared to 11.1 percent and 12.5 percent in 1995 and 1996, respectively). The data for 1998 (as compared to December 1997) are not encouraging: real GDP 2 percent, CPI 12 percent, unemployment 14 percent. National Statistical Institute, Sofia, and communication with M. Wyzan, IIASA, Vienna, May 1998. It should be mentioned here that the CPI for the first three quarters of 1998 (December 1997 = 100) for some services increased so much as for example: rents − 138.8 percent, transport and communications − 100.9 percent, medical services − 142.5 percent, dentist − 134.5 percent, education and leisure − 18.7 percent, theater, cinema, sports − 139.3 percent.

3. The internal debt of Bulgarian firms increased in 1998 by 40 percent and approximately 50 percent of the trade turnover is in barter (*Sega*, no.4 [157], January 28–February 3, 1999, p. 36).

4. The trade balance and the current account balance deteriorated in 1998 (respectively negative by 132 mio.$ and 93 mio.$). It is estimated that in 1999 the figures would be respectively 445 mio.$ and 380 mio$, rising to more than 500 mio.$ each in the years 2000 and 2001. (*Sega*, no.5 [158], February 4–10, 1999, p. 27 and own estimates). Balance of payments adjustments giving the large short-term external debt (more than 1 bio.$) are needed, leading to increased borrowing and net external debt. The war on the peninsula will further worsen the external balance of Bulgaria in the next two years. (See for detailed data on Bulgaria's key economic indicators in 1997–2000 the quarterly reports of Plan Econ, Inc., Washington, D.C.).

REFERENCES

Bruno, Michael. (1993). *Crisis, Stabilization, and Economic Reform. Therapy by Consensus*. Clarendon Press, Oxford.

Fischer, Stanley. (1996). "Maintaining Price Stability." *Finance and Development*, December, pp. 34–37.

Keynes, J. M. (1988). *The Economic Consequences of the Peace*. Harmondsworth, Penguin (first published 1919).

Zloch-Christy, Iliana, ed. (1996). *Bulgaria in a Time of Change. Economic and Political Dimensions*. Avebury, Aldershot, UK.

Conclusion: What Have We Learned?

Iliana Zloch-Christy

This book has attempted to analyze economic policy in postcommunist Eastern Europe with special attention focused on the financial arrangement of currency boards. The transforming countries in the region are trying to join the integrated world economy. They opened their economies after 1989 in terms of more open exchange rate policies and exchange controls, and no prohibitive tariffs and quotas, and they are facing the challenge of finding strategic alliances and attracting foreign capital. Their economic development varies accross countries and depends on institution building (private property and market-based trade), geography (for example, their proximity to Western markets and their natural endowments), history, culture, norms, values, and human capital.

The contributors to the volume agree that success in the process of institution building is one of the most important factors for the transformation process and development strategy in the individual countries in the region. They adhere strongly to a positive approach in their analysis. In assessing the impact of the currency boards arrangement on the domestic economy different views are presented. While Iikka Korhonen, Pekka Sutela, Niina Pautola, Vello Vensel, and Mart Sörg in their analyses come to the conclusion that the impact has been positive, Iliana Zloch-Christy is highly critical in the chapter on Bulgaria. My main arguments are that in a situation of *repressed depreciation*, given the fixed exchange rate, the recessionary effect on the economy should not be underestimated and underscores the following:

1. the appreciation in real terms of the domestic currency with the negative impact on the country's exports and competitiveness.
2. the deterioration of the trade and current account balances.
3. urgent need of balance-of-payments financing, overborrowing and further deterioration of the country's external balance.
4. real income decline, given the downward pressure on the value of the currency, and adjustments are lengthy and costly in terms of both output and employment.

In addition, it should be also stressed that currency boards slowed down the reform process in the Eastern European countries that adopted it, since in these countries both the experience in designing and conducting monetary policy and the availability of monetary policy instruments are limited. And the fiscal policy making under the currency board is not necessarily more prudent.

G. Kolodko in his analysis stresses the importance of institution building and the fact that the course of events in postcommunist Eastern Europe has been under great pressure from policies based upon the Washington consensus. But it is also true that the transition to a market economy and occurrences accompanying this process have had a significant impact upon the revision of these policies. On the one hand, the line of thought typical for the Washington consensus has had important meaning for the directions of systemic reform and policy attempts in Eastern Europe and the former Soviet Union. The fact that suggested and executed policies did not bring the expected results led to a search for alternative policy means. Actually, the range of issues upon which there is consensus among the major partners on the global financial, economic, and political scene has expanded over the last years. Kolodko stresses in his analysis that the transition to a market economy is a lengthy process comprised of various spheres of economic activities. The naive belief that a market economy can be introduced by "shock therapy" is wrong, and in several cases, when attempted, has caused more problems than it has solved. Because a market economy requires adequate institutional structures and appropriate behavior, transition can be executed only in a gradual manner, since these are gradual processes based on new organizations, new laws, and the changing behavior of various economic entities.

In 1989, influential financial organizations, political bodies, and professional economists seemed to agree on the main points for economic policy reform. This was termed the Washington consensus. Despite the fact that the economic policy of the Washington consensus was initially developed without any concern for postsocialist transformation, these ideas have significantly influenced the path of thought and action in Eastern Europe and the former Soviet Union. Because these policies were not intended for the overhaul of postcommunist countries, however, they have failed.

A new, post-Washington consensus is developing, as it should, based on the lessons learned from experience thus far. Some major policy conclusions can be drawn:

- Institutional arrangements are the most important factor for progress toward durable growth.
- Policy must recognize that institution building by its nature must be a gradual process.
- Policy makers must acknowledge that the size of the government is less important than the quality of its policy and the manner of the changes of government dimension.
- If institutional arrangement is neglected and left to the spontaneous processes and unleashed forces of liberalized markets, then informal institutionalization fills the systemic vacuum.
- In transition economies policies must transform and streamline the judiciary system to serve the market economy.
- A shift of competence and power from the central government to local governments is necessary for deregulation of the postsocialist economy.
- There is an urgent need to accelerate the development of non-government organizations.
- During transition income policy and government concern for equitable growth should have great meaning.
- Short-term capital liberalization must be monitored and controlled by the countries' fiscal and monetary authorities with the support of international financial institutions.

- The Bretton Woods organizations should reconsider their policies toward transition economies aiming at institutional building and support for equitable growth.

It is probably too early to assess the impact of currency boards on the economic development of the countries that adopted them in Eastern Europe in the 1990s. The chapters in this volume do not discuss issues regarding where future economic and political developments may go in the transition economies. We hope that the reader will be better served by the positive analysis in this volume than by works speculating on future development.

Select Bibliography

Balino, Tomas J. T., and Charles Enoch, eds. (1997). *Currency Boards Arrangements. Issues and Experiences.* International Monetary Fund, Washington, D.C.

Frenkel, Jacob A., ed. (1991). *International Financial Policy. Essays in Honor of Jacques J. Polak*, International Monetary Fund, Washington, D.C.

Kwan, Yum K., and Francis T. Liu. (1996). *Hong Kong's Currency Board and Changing Monetary Regimes.* National Bureau of Economic Research working paper, no. 5723, Cambridge, Mass.

Perry, Guillermo E., ed. (1996). *Currency Boards and External Shocks. How Much Pain, How Much Gain?* World Bank, Washington, D.C.

Romer, Christina D. and David H. (1996). *Institutions for Monetary Stability.* National Bureau of Economic Research working paper, no. 5557, Cambridge, Mass.

Williamson, John. (1995). *What Role for Currency Boards?* Institute for International Economics, Washington, D.C.

Zloch-Christy, Iliana, ed. (1998). *Eastern Europe and the World Economy. Challenges of Transition and Globalization.* E. Elgar Publishing, U.K.

Index

About the Editor and Contributors

RICHARD N. COOPER, Maurits C. Boas Professor of International Economics, Department of Economics, Harvard University.

GRZEGORZ W. KOLODKO, Department of Economics, Warsaw University and former first deputy prime minister and minister of finance, Poland.

IIKKA KORHONEN, National Bank of Finland.

NIINA PAUTOLA, National Bank of Finland and Helsinki School of Economics.

PEKKA SUTELA, Director, Institute for Russian and East European Studies, National Bank of Finland.

MART SÖRG, University of Tartu.

VELLO VENSEL, Technical University of Tallin, Estonia.

ILIANA ZLOCH-CHRISTY, economist and former faculty associate, Department of Economics, Harvard University, and St. Antony's College, Oxford University.

ISBN 0-275-96858-8
90000>
EAN
9 780275 968588
HARDCOVER BAR CODE